PRINCIPLE CENTERED SELLING

THIS BOOK WILL HELP YOU
DEFINE OR REDEFINE
WHAT IT MEANS TO BE A
PROFESSIONAL SALESPERSON.

RANDY SOBEL

Principle Centered Selling

Sobel University

PO Box 65002
University Place, WA 98464
Tel: (253) 565-2577
Fax: (253) 565-2768
www.sobeluniversity.com

ORDERING INFORMATION

Quantity Sales:
Special discounts are available on quantity purchases by corporations, associations and others. For details contact the "Special Sales Department" at the address above.

Individual Sales:
Sobel University Publications are available through most bookstores. They can also be ordered directly from Sobel University by following the contact information above.

COURSE INFORMATION

For continuing education or to get caught up on what is current and relevant since you last attended class visit www.sobeluniversity.com

Library of Congress Control Number: 2014916647
ISBN-13: 978-0-9908220-1-1

www.sobeluniversity.com

Printed in U.S.A

*This book is dedicated
to the thousands of students
who have asked for this
training tool to be put
in writing.*

*You're the motivation
that has inspired the efforts
to create this book.*

CONTENTS

Read This First!

LET'S GET STARTED

Principle Centered Selling means that when a salesperson speaks to a client their words are guided by what they truly believe. This reveals that principles guide our behaviors when no one is looking. As a new or experienced salesperson, sales manager or business owner, the principles in this book will serve as a road map, game plan or job description when navigating the selling process. This book will point out what top producers do to ensure success and the non-productive challenges that must be controlled and addressed.

TO BE A PRINCIPLE IN THIS BOOK, IT MUST MEET THE FOLLOWING EXACT CRITERIA:

1. All principles must be a catalyst to make sales.

2. Each principle is required to be able to stand alone on its own merits.

3. Each principle cannot violate another principle.

4. A principle can complement another principle, but still must be able to stand alone.

This book is written for salespeople who want to get paid what they are worth. Commission is the best friend of any sales professional as it has no limits. When a salesperson wants to make more, they learn more skills and get paid for their efforts by increasing their closing ratio. Top salespeople know that they can only speak to a definite number of clients in a day so they have to do their best with each opportunity.

This book is also written for sales managers and owners whose very existence in their business is determined by the productivity of their sales team. The challenge that many leaders face is that they were never top-producing salespeople prior to becoming managers, and even if they were, they may not have the skills to teach sales properly.

This book is also written to help leaders more quickly identify the traits and characteristics of top salespeople. The principles may become part of your interview process to be sure that your newly hired salesperson and manager have agreed to the same selling philosophy and rules of your business culture. Salespeople may use this book the same way when making a decision about the quality of a manager or company before they accept a job or a new selling career.

This book is also written for professionals in sales who recognize that selling today is different, and it will be ever-changing in the future. As the internet has changed the way consumers shop, research and finally purchase, salespeople must adapt their presentations to take into account these new clients' types. Old sales lines and slick tactics are not tolerated by today's consumers. Not to mention, that in seconds, they let everyone they know how they feel they have been treated.

This book will help you define or redefine your belief in what selling is all about. As the title indicates, Principle Centered Selling is more a book about helping people buy though a moral value-based approach with a compass always pointing toward the close of the sale. The principles will support that your clients already came in to make a purchase and simply require you to be their teacher and help them purchase.

As everything in life is sales, the examples in this book come from everywhere. As you read about a selling step, process or technique, try to replace the product in the example with your own. The principles will fit all selling organizations with minor adaptations as they are mostly universal truths. For example, the principles will cover everything from the importance of building a client base to what you say and how you deliver your message to your clients. The principles will also serve as a guide to help you stay on track throughout your entire selling process.

One of the chief motivators for writing this book came from years of asking sales professionals a particular question. How many of you, when you were young, dreamed about being a salesperson when you grew up? The young kid version of you probably said you wanted to be a fireman, a doctor, a train conductor, a pilot, but never a salesperson. Since very few people grew up thinking that they wanted to be a salesperson, their career path and courses they studied did not prepare them for being a professional salesperson.

Many students at Sobel University have advanced degrees in many other disciplines, but not sales. The selling principles written in this book are also part of the core material taught at Sobel University. Like any other profession, selling requires a very specific set of skills that are learned and can be mastered with the right instruction and study time. Skill-based schools are aimed at putting people to work with the aptitude needed to perform now. This is what Sobel University is to the world of sales professionals.

Professional salespeople are easily recognized by the consumers. They have been trained with the proper education and have the qualifications to do the job. This allows them the confidence to help provide the highest level of customer service. It is unfortunate when salespeople are asked to perform without the skills. Untrained salespeople lead to turnover and financial stress for all people working in a sales organization and the results of this are easily recognized and felt by your clients. This book will help you learn and identify what it takes to become a top-producing sales professional.

As this book is written for Sobel University students as well as all professionals in sales, a worksheet is provided at the end of each chapter. These worksheets are designed to stimulate thought about your personal application of each principle while developing a plan to put the principle to work in your business.

The principles in this book have been incorporated in many business plans and mission statements. They have been used for personal training, in sales meetings, selling shows, spousal interviews, presented to youth groups, at business owner conventions as well as presented at many business schools. Through the understanding and application of these principles, a better quality of salesperson is being equipped with the skills to excel in a great profession.

Once you have read the principles in this book, your perception of what it means to be a professional salesperson will change forever. Professional sales has always been a well-kept secret hidden behind the stigma of how poorly trained salespeople present the industry. As this is one of the last places where you can truly get paid what you are worth, the result is more quality and educated people are flocking to a professional sales career. This book is great for getting continuing education with current and relevant sales skills, and is the best place to start if you are new to sales.

Finally, to get the most out of this book, read each principle as if you have never been in sales or purchased anything from a salesperson. This will be the most difficult challenge in the book. If you are trying to relate the principle you are reading to what you know or have experienced, it may get in the way of receiving the new message. The Start With An Empty Head Principle that you will read about later will expose the hazards of combining two good concepts and ending with a diluted or watered down, ineffective presentation. As you read through the book, try to take some time after each principle to reflect on its particular meaning, application to your business, and how it will play into your life.

ONE

THE GRAPH

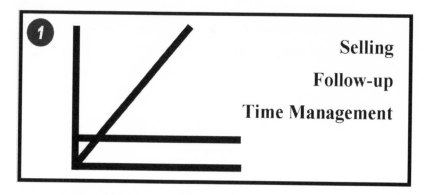

This first chapter will address the quality of your clients. Why does it always seem that some salespeople always have higher closing ratios than others? Why does it also seem that top salespeople work less and make more? In this chapter, we will explore and reveal their secret in a way that anyone can use to replicate their success. To be equipped to explain the formula of top producers the following diagrams below will serve as reference points.

THE EQUATION:

_____ Number of clients per day

x_____ Number of days worked per month

=_____ Clients per month

x_____ Closing Ratio

=_____ Number of sales per month

x_____ Average commission

=_____ Monthly income

Looking at "The Equation," start filling it out with your own information. Begin with the number of clients you speak to in an average day. This may be more difficult with seasonal businesses. If it turns out that you speak to fewer people on a Wednesday in February than you would on a Saturday in June, you can adjust your numbers, or better yet, start target marketing[1] efforts to balance out your opportunities.

Next, multiply by the number of days you work per month. Try to use your real number and include when you come in on your days off. This could include days that your client can only make it on your day off, covering for coworkers who are away for training, making up for an incorrectly staffed dealership, off-site sales, or other special sales or promotions. The total will tell you the number of clients you speak to in a month. As you go use this equation, try to make this number as consistent as possible. You will find that talking to more clients will not increase your closing ratio; in fact, it will have the opposite effect.

Going back to "The Equation," you will now insert your real closing ratio. This could be a difficult number to find if it is not tracked accurately. Pressure from management or incorrect advice from trainers can lead you to using a number that is too high. This always reveals itself when you get to the bottom and look at your monthly income. At the bottom, if all of the other numbers are correct, you can go back and adjust your closing ratio based on your real monthly income.

---

1   A target market is a group of individual end users of your product. Your job when there is no traffic is to bring your product to your market

The next number you will be looking at is your total number of sales per month. If this is too high or low then simply go back and adjust your closing ratio.

The next multiplier is your average commission. This is an easy number to find. Take your paycheck and divide it by the number of sales per month. Always remember to take your total pay amount even if there are salaries, guarantees or bonuses. You must make the assumption that without the sales, you would not have the other pay.

Finally you arrive at your monthly income. To check for accuracy, multiply your monthly income times twelve. If this is close to your annual income, you have done a good job at filling in your equation accurately. If it is not close, you need to go back and make the necessary corrections. It is not uncommon to keep two equations in the beginning for seasonal natured business. Later, when you have built your client base, you will see the seasonal differences become less substantial.

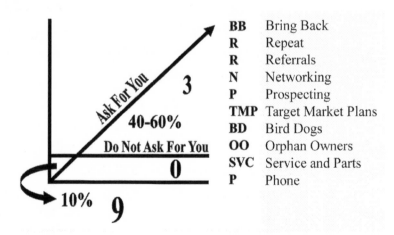

BB	Bring Back
R	Repeat
R	Referrals
N	Networking
P	Prospecting
TMP	Target Market Plans
BD	Bird Dogs
OO	Orphan Owners
SVC	Service and Parts
P	Phone

The Graph has two major elements that drive its function. First is where it shows the level line above the baseline that has typed: Do Not Ask For You. This refers to first time clients you have never met before. These are the clients who may have been shopping you five states away on the internet, or who may have just had a bad experience with another salesperson that they did not purchase from. These clients probably don't know you, like you, or even trust you. Last night, they may have heard a comedian tell jokes about your job, and they are possibly afraid that you will take advantage of their desire to purchase. You can't build a client base from just waiting at the front door for your next opportunity.

Years ago, I met a salesperson in my class who was a real stand-out. He sat in the front, participated actively and was correct most of the time. Later I told his manager that he was a real pleasure to have in class and, with his more than 30 years in the business, he must be one of their top producers. The manager quickly corrected me and said, "Are you talking about Dave? He's consistently one of our weakest producers. Did he tell you he had thirty years in the business or that he had one year in the business thirty times?" That was the manager's way of saying that the salesperson started over every day and never built a client base.

From that manager's quote I was better able to understand the concept of becoming a drug addict to the front door. There is a way to define the word "addict" that is helpful: a person who is in a perpetual belief they are in need of an activity or habit to the point of becoming physiologically or psychologically reliant. Wow. I thought that it was only my manager's fault for telling salespeople to "not worry about the last one and go get another," or "if you don't think a fresh client is valuable, then try living without one for 30 days." No matter what the reason, this drug addiction to fresh clients gets in the way of building a client base. This is serious and real! It also has been known to put a strain on quality family time; if you become addicted to fresh clients, you may not make it to family events on time, and then eventually, not at all!

This addiction is hard to break. Every day, there are other salespeople encouraging you to not leave your place waiting for clients at the front door. Strong words like, "They are flooding the floor" or "Don't hire more salespeople. We can handle the traffic," are empowering the addiction problem.

Getting back to The Graph, the numbers below the base line refer to an example of a salesperson with a front door addiction problem. The 10% closing ratio, or losing nine times out of ten, is not a very desirable job success rate. If you were to apply the 10% to your equation, you may be shocked to find that you may be suffering from an addiction problem too. Unfortunately, some salespeople adjust their lifestyle to this low income and get stuck here forever.

Before we can get to the second part of The Graph, let's understand how to break this addiction. Starting with basic statistics will help make the point. If you flip a coin 100 times in a row and it comes up with heads each and every time, what are the odds that it will be tails on the next flip? I hope you said 50%. The odds don't change with each flip of the coin.

Let's try that again. What if the odds of winning the lottery are 1 in 7,000,000 (slightly higher if you don't play) and you purchase 7,000,000 computer-generated lottery tickets. What are your odds of winning now? I hope you said 1 in 7,000,000 per ticket and that the odds don't change.

If this makes sense with statistics, let's see if we can apply it to your business. What if I worked for you for 30 years with a 10% closing ratio, and I just lost 9 times in a row at the front door. What will be my closing ratio with the next client I speak to with this 30 year track record? Wow, I sure hope all of you said 10%. This is a frustrating statistic for business owners. It is as if you told them to take their advertising cost per unit sold and place it as a bet on a wheel in Las Vegas with a one in ten chance of winning.

Knowing clearly that waiting at the front door is not the desired way to build a client base, let's break free of that paradigm. Starting with the client you have just helped, let's change a behavior. Rather than not worrying about that one and just getting another, let's go on the offense. To do this, you must understand that times have changed. Not even ten years ago, if a client liked you and wanted you to follow-up with them, they would have given you their home phone number. If you called them, it was likely that they were not home and probably more likely that they were out shopping your competition. The best you could have expected was to leave a message and hope that you were the first and possibly the only one to follow-up with them that day.

With cell phones, the last example has become extinct. Today if a client really likes you they will give you their cell number for follow-up rather than their home number even if they still have a home phone. This sets you up for the first follow-up call. Picture the conversation your clients are having on their way to their car to leave. They may look at each other and confirm that they liked you, the product, and the business. If they were given an A+ presentation, they really don't want to start over with another salesperson. Then, while they are just getting in their car to leave, you call.

"As I was walking back to my desk, I was just thinking about what a pleasure it was to meet both of you. It was really great that we both raise basset hounds and have had similar experiences with them. Before I set your file down and start with a new client, again I just want to thank you for coming in and express the great pleasure I had in helping you. I did think of some other products to show you on your next visit."

Then pause and wait for a response. If they had a chance to confirm that you, your product and your business were where they want to purchase, they could get out and come back inside. After all, the prospect of starting over again with another salesperson is not too attractive if they already like you. The question you have to ask yourself with this example is: How many of the nine out of ten that you just lost with will come back in? By the numbers, if just one comes back in, your sales double! If you are sincere and not pushy, you may be surprised at how many clients want to stop shopping and purchase now.

*Top salespeople build The Graph
with a goal of being totally
independent of the front door.
They call this independence
being "UP FREE."*

Moving forward on The Graph, let's look at the line moving up at a 45 degree angle. It is labeled ASK FOR YOU. This refers to the clients who come in and ask for you by name. These clients know you, the product, the business, and most likely the price range of what they are looking to purchase. With this group of buyers you can expect a very high closing ratio. The example in The Graph shows a 40-60% closing ratio, but this author believes it to be much higher.

Now put the 40% or 60% closing ratio in your own equation and see what your income would be if you only spoke with clients who asked for you. The list on the right side of The Graph going down the page refers to some of the people who could ask for you. The list starts with clients your bring back, repeat, referral, networking, prospecting and so on. While this book is not dedicated to just The Graph, volumes of books could be written only on the topic of how to build a client base. Building a client base is a critical key to unlocking the other important principles.

In your business, you must determine how long a quality presentation takes to deliver. Then you must allow time for follow-up, or you will never become "UP FREE." Businesses that are understaffed promote drug-like addiction to standing at the front door. If you know that it takes 2-5 hours to present your product in a way that your client will feel empowered to purchase, you can only give 1-2 presentations per day and still have time to build your client base.

An unavoidable fact is that the least productive salespeople have the largest pool of fresh customers. While the top producers are speaking to a single client for 2-5 hours, the least skilled salespeople may speak to two to four clients in the same time period. Most business have a merit-based rotation to help manage the traffic flow and allow for a more productive model. The two examples of this that follow are customized to their individual industries.

Two of our clients have put Systems in place to combat this occurrence in their respective industries. One client will only allow their salespeople to speak with one new client per day and they staff accordingly. Another client will only allow their salespeople to speak with new prospects for their first five years working in their business. Their logic is that if you have not built The Graph by then and become "UP FREE," the business is better off starting over with a new salesperson who is willing to do the job.

Now back to the principle, The Graph. What has been established this far is that you can expect a low closing ratio and a much more challenging selling process from fresh walk-in clients who do not ask for you. Conversely, if you only help clients who come in and ask for you, your life will be much easier. To accomplish this, "UP FREE" sales career, there are three factors that you must manage and control.

First, you must have a solid follow-up system. Your follow-up system must organize and prioritize your leads and prospects. It must be integrated with a management system so that help is readily available, and you can be observed and counseled. Your system must have a way to collect the information from your client to provide follow-up beyond their level of expectation. It must have a game plan for before and after the sale. And finally, it must be easily accessible when a client calls, or for future walk-in sales years later. At buyers' clinics, one of my favorite pieces of advice that I give to shoppers is to ask the salesperson to show their follow-up system. I follow that by saying that if they don't intend to follow-up with you and take care of your needs after the sale, leave.

Second, you must have a solid selling system. You can have the best follow-up in the world, but if your sales tactics are old, insulting, pushy, or otherwise unprofessional, no one will take your follow-up call. Your selling system must be free of all slick lines that your client heard at the last place, where they didn't purchase. Other upcoming principles in this book will help drive this point home.

And finally, third, you must have an exceptional time management system. Having a great follow-up system along with a great selling system is useless without time management. Many salespeople say, "Today is the day I will start doing follow-up correctly." They sit down at their phone and start to call prospective clients. Just when they think they are on the right track, a manager comes up to them and says, "Who is helping those people over there?" They set aside the follow-up and head toward the fresh walk in client to continue to feed their front door addiction. Having a set time for follow-up will allow you to capitalize on both follow-up as well as the front door.

The last part of The Graph that has not been addressed are the numbers 3 in the middle of The Graph and the 0 toward the bottom of The Graph. These numbers represent your ultimate goal on your best days. What if you could put the 3 into the equation next to the clients you talk to per day, and they were all from the top part of The Graph, clients who ask for you. And if the 0 represents you not speaking to any fresh clients on that same day, you probably had a very productive day if you follow the math to the bottom of the equation.

The Graph represents your goal of becoming "UP FREE!" As with any goal, start with the first step and measure your progress. This is a large goal, so it may be easier to start with a goal of having an appointment every other day. Build it to an appointment every day. Go as many consecutive days as you can with one appointment per day. Then start adding a second appointment per day. By this time you will be well on your way to mastering The Graph Principle.

Putting The Graph Principle To Work

The following questions are designed to gain a working understanding and real application in your business and in your life. Always try to answer the following questions before moving on to the next principle. This will provide you the opportunity to reflect on the value of each principle as a standalone concept. The more quality effort you apply to your answers, the better chance you will see immediate and lasting results from the value of each principle. The questions below are the same at the end of each chapter. Being cognizant of this will allow you to develop an action plan for putting the principles to work as you continue to read.

Define the key points of this principle that you will apply in your business.

Give an example of how the author demonstrated the principle.

Write three real examples of what you would say to your clients to show how you can apply this principle in your business.

Define three plans to exemplify ways that this principle will increase the quality of your selling process, margins, volume, and relationship with your clients.

Write an analogy of how this principle would apply outside of business.

TWO

DE-CAN YOUR PRESENTATION

 De-Can your presentation.

Speak in analogy.

The goal of this principle is to learn your presentation and product so well that you can speak in analogy. This is exemplified by the simple way we ask our clients how they want to pay. While all of the following questions are correct, the only one you should use is the one that fits how your client best listens and comprehends. "How would you like to handle the balance, pay cash or finance?" "How did you want to handle the balance, pay cash or make payments?" "Were you thinking you want to make payments or pay cash?" "Y'all thinkin' you wanted to cash me on out of this, or make notes?"

While there are many more ways to ask the same question, the only correct way is the way your client will feel comfortable hearing your words. Yes, words matter! In a financial part of town, the word finance will work well. In more rural and suburban parts of town, the word payment will fit the way more clients will want to hear you ask. And in parts of the south, you may have to ask if they were planning on making notes.

When you deliver your presentations, try to think of the old Jay Leno comedy sketch, "Jaywalking." He would go out to the streets and ask what would appear to be the most obvious questions and get the strangest answers. I often wondered what the answers would be if he asked, "What is a lien holder?" Would the responses be, "Someone who leans and holds. Like holding sheetrock against a wall while waiting for someone to nail it down."

Keep your language simple. So many people think they need to use big words that make them sound impressive. These unctuous pettifogging voracious ruminate carbon creatures can easily come off as pompous as the fictional characters Fraiser and Niles Crane. Try to remember that the number one selling newspaper in the world boasts that it writes at the sixth-grade level. Keep your words simple and your language clear for all to understand.

The part of this principle that is most confusing is that we have to build our presentation for our clients. For so many years, the belief has been that we need to change our presentation so that we don't sound like robots. Many sales professionals believe that they need to change the working presentation into their own words so that they can feel good delivering the message. These concepts miss the mark. If you have a working presentation, why change what works just because you don't like a word or two? And why is it important how we feel when we aren't the ones spending our hard-earned money? Remember to build your presentation for your clients.

Next, let's address the purpose of speaking in analogy. Have you ever delivered a message to someone and you could clearly see from their expression they didn't understand? So, promptly you changed the words and they still didn't understand. Finally, you changed the words again and halfway through your delivery, they interrupted you to say, "I get it, I know what you mean." This is why we need to know our material so well that we can deliver the message multiple ways without losing the meaning.

A common mistake would be to change the message before it is needed. Many of your presentations are set up to work with material that may not be delivered for hours. If you change the delivery of your presentation, you may leave out critical information that is needed at the end to put it all together. This would be as if you left out critical clues from a murder mystery and the solution did not make sense at the end.

On a final note, de-canning your presentation and learning to speak in analogy are only needed when your client is not able to follow your standard presentation. We do not need to change our working presentation just because we used it with the last client who purchased. Long successful running plays on Broadway do not change the script because the actor gets bored delivering the play night after night. Remember, your presentation is always new to the next client!

Putting The De-Can Your Presentation Principle to Work

The following questions are designed to gain a working understanding and real application in your business and in your life. Always try to answer the following questions before moving on to the next principle. This will provide you the opportunity to reflect on the value of each principle as a standalone concept. The more quality effort you apply to your answers, the better chance you will see immediate and lasting results from the value of each principle. The questions below are the same at the end of each chapter. Being cognizant of this will allow you to develop an action plan for putting the principles to work as you continue to read.

Define the key points of this principle that you will apply in your business.

Give an example of how the author demonstrated the principle.

Write three real examples of what you would say to your clients to show how you can apply this principle in your business.

Define three plans to exemplify ways that this principle will increase the quality of your selling process, margins, volume, and relationship with your clients.

Write an analogy of how this principle would apply outside of business.

31

THREE

Sell By Compartments

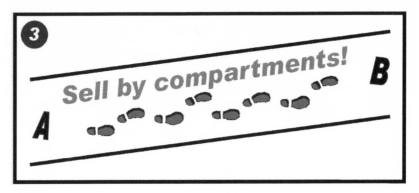

Picture a road that has undrivable conditions on either side of it. The road may be twenty feet wide but with the hazards on each side you want to stay toward the middle of the road to stay safe. So if we tie this to geometry, the quickest and safest way down the road would be in a straight line: Point A to Point B. If your selling process road is similar, you have to be prepared for when the client does not stay in the middle of the road. One example would be when a client comes into your business and before you get a chance to say one word, they say: "I don't want any of your salesperson stuff. I've been to five other businesses and shopped yours online. What's your best price on that one over there (as they point to one of your products)?" Using the geometry as tool, let's look at the three options that a salesperson has available and then select the strategy that will work.

Option One: If your client is demanding your best price and has in fact shopped at five other businesses, one training company would tell you to give them a price and go for the close. That company believes that every client must be served up a price. They believe that without giving the client a price, you will never make the sale. To sum up option one would be to acknowledge that any client who has shopped online and been to five other businesses is ready to buy; they just need a price from you.

Option Two: According to the laws of geometry the quickest way back to the road you want to be on (the one that runs down the middle in a straight and direct way from point A to point B) would be a straight line from where you are to the proper road. This straight line would form a right angle. So if you are halfway down the road and find that you are heading in the wrong direction, this option suggests that you turn sharply to make a direct line to the correct road. It frequently sounds like this: "It sound like you have done a lot of shopping. If I could get you the product you are looking for at the lowest price, could I earn your business today?" This option suggests that wherever you are in the selling process you can proceed on once you get a commitment that your client will buy if the numbers are correct.

Option Three: According to the laws of geometry once you leave Point A, the only way back is to follow your direct path back. That was Hansel and Gretel's strategy as they dropped bread crumbs to find their way back home as they entered the forest. This option suggests that the only way to make the sale is to go back to the beginning and follow all the steps correctly and stay in the middle of the road of your selling process.

Now it is time to choose your path. Option one, where you give the client a price and go for the close? Option two, where you "If I Could, Would You" and continue? Or option three, where you go back to the beginning and follow all of your steps in your selling process? After years of asking this question to thousands of salespeople throughout the U.S. and Canada, it is still shocking that all three answers are still selected.

The correct option can best be found by first dismissing the two that will not work. Start with option one. If you serve up a price and your price is the best your client has seen so far, then they will say, "Well, we keep shopping and the prices keep getting lower, therefore we should keep shopping." If you give a price that is too high or higher than they have seen elsewhere they will say, "Your prices aren't even competitive, we're leaving." It's not so funny to watch a salesperson ask these clients what other prices they have heard because the response goes like this, "It wouldn't be fair to the other salesperson to tell you their price." This client's response leaves you wanting to tell the client that what they are doing is not exactly fair either. Option one does not work because if your price is too high or too low the client leaves.

Option two does not work for the same reasons. This option states that we get a commitment that the client will purchase if the numbers are correct. Unfortunately this assumption leaves too much out of the equation. First it assumes that the previous salesperson built enough of a relationship in the meet and greet step for the client to give them accurate information. Next, it assumes that the last salesperson selected the right product that fits the client's wants, needs, and budget. It also assumes that the last salesperson presented and demonstrated the product correctly. This list of assumptions can go on and on but it is safe to say that if the last salesperson did everything correctly they would have made the sale. Option two is not a reasonable possible solution.

Option three is the correct answer. Since the client is in front of you, we can conclude that everything was not done correctly during any previous presentations. Since we don't know what the last salesperson did wrong, we must start at the beginning. There is an old saying in sales: If we knew why the client didn't buy, we would have fixed it and made the sale.

So the title of this principle is Sell By Compartments. If you break down the steps in the Road to the Sale into compartments, and then complete each step before moving to the next, the third option of the story delivers the message. The reason that option three, going back to the beginning, is the only effective option is because nothing is left to assumption.

If a Road to the Sale starts with meet and greet, and your goals in this step are clearly defined and you accomplish or surpass your goals, then you are ready to move to the next step. If your next step is product selection, and you accomplish or surpass your goals, then you are ready to move to the next step. This continues throughout the selling process. A word of caution:

Be sure your goals are clear, measurable, attainable and easily communicated to coworkers, subordinates, supervisors and most of all, your clients.

The objective of this principle:
DO NOT MOVE ON TO THE NEXT STEP UNTIL YOU HAVE COMPLETED YOUR GOALS IN THE PREVIOUS STEP.

SIMPLY PUT:
How can you write up a deal if the
client doesn't like the product?

Why would you present a product if you don't know
if it fits your client's wants, needs or budget?

Why would you think a client would trust you and
give you truthful information if you don't take the
time to build a safe place to communicate?

Another way to say the goal of this principle:
DO NOT MOVE ON TO THE NEXT STEP BEFORE YOU HAVE COMPLETED THE PREVIOUS STEP.

The two definitions are similar however the words until and before are interchangeable. These words are critical as they show the order and sequencing of events. Managers have said this in meeting after meeting, and I say it here again: Don't skip steps!

Putting Sell By Compartments Principle to Work

The following questions are designed to gain a working understanding and real application in your business and in your life. Always try to answer the following questions before moving on to the next principle. This will provide you the opportunity to reflect on the value of each principle as a standalone concept. The more quality effort you apply to your answers, the better chance you will see immediate and lasting results from the value of each principle. The questions below are the same at the end of each chapter. Being cognizant of this will allow you to develop an action plan for putting the principles to work as you continue to read.

Define the key points of this principle that you will apply in your business.

Give an example of how the author demonstrated the principle.

Write three real examples of what you would say to your clients to show how you can apply this principle in your business.

Define three plans to exemplify ways that this principle will increase the quality of your selling process, margins, volume, and relationship with your clients.

Write an analogy of how this principle would apply outside of business.

FOUR

SCALE OF THE SALE

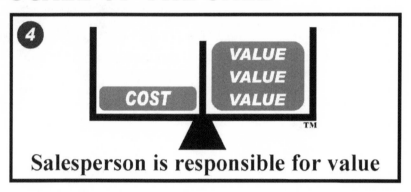

Salesperson is responsible for value

This principle implies that we are weighing valuable concepts on a scale. To be more accurate, we are putting a weight and comparison to Cost versus Value. We all know that when Value outweighs Cost in our client's mind they will purchase our products. Unfortunately in this internet-shopping competitive marketplace each Cost and Value must be defined more clearly.

Starting with Cost, many of our clients think it is their right to know what we paid for our products and what they should pay us in profit. Who gave the clients this idea? Maybe all the businesses who advertise: ONLY PAY INVOICE, $1.00 OVER INVOICE SALE, ONLY PAY WHAT WE PAY SALE or BUY AT OUR COST SALE! What if the ads read: BUSINESSES THAT DON'T MAKE PROFIT WILL BE OUT OF BUSINESS or BUSINESSES CAN'T MAKE UP FOR LOSING MONEY BY DOING VOLUME - - THEY JUST LOSE MORE!

Have we trained our clients to expect to pay less? To make the necessary paradigm shift we have to understand our true cost. As presenter at many buying shows over many years, retail clients have asked the same question over and over again: "How do we know how much the seller is making when we purchase their product?" The answer is surprisingly easily explained and accepted. First the question is turned back to the audience to list the costs involved in running the business to include: taxes, insurance, payroll, minimum factory orders, employee benefits, rent, equipment, tools, and of course, all the inventory. So the correct answer to how much does the seller make when they sell me their product is: We don't know. Most businesses don't know how much they make until the end of the year, quarter, or selling season. Businesses have to speculate or forecast sales and the margins needed against projected expenses. If they guess right they make money; if they guess wrong they lose money. It is that simple.

The above is easily comprehended by clients when they think of the business where they work. Sometimes, you have to say to the client, "If a business tells you they are not making money on the sale of their product, leave now. They are either lying, or will be out of business soon and will not be there to take care of you after the sale." It's also acceptable to say, "Our business will make money or will not sell you the product. Without a profit we would not be here." The truth is always the correct thing to say. It is easy to understand and accept.

On the Cost side of the scale sometimes we have to deal with competitors from many states away offering a low internet price. This is nothing new. Even in the old days of newspaper ads and competitors across town, someone was always trying to get rid of their old aged inventory or increase market share. While it is frustrating that your new ten-day-old inventory is competing with your competitors' same model that is three hundred days old, this situation will always exist. As for your competition that is simply trying to increase market share by selling for less, know there is a limit to how much they are willing to lose.

Before we leave the Cost side of the scale, we must identify our most satisfied clients. This is a universal truth and a self-fulfilling prophecy: "The clients who pay us the most profit are the most satisfied." When a client pays your retail asking price you are in a position to give them great service after the sale. Conversely, if a client negotiates you down to the last penny, you will have no profit or reserve to be able to provide service after the sale. When you make money, the client gets great service before, during, and after the sale because you can afford to provide service at that level.

So what is Cost on the scale? It is the number at which your business wishes to sell the product. Therefore, Cost equals Full Retail. That means that as salespeople we are not empowered to sell the product for a dime more or less than full retail. Our business set the price based on the expenses listed above and fair market value of the product. Since our product price is fixed, the only variable we have any say in will be if we can help the client to see that the Value exceeds the Cost on the scale. In other chapters we will address the exceptions for when we should sell for more or less.

Since Cost is set, let's start addressing the Value side of the scale. In the chapter titled Interactive Presentation, the Value side of the scale will be explained in detail. However, there are some factors that must be addressed now. First, ask yourself, have you ever been given a perfect presentation on a product? Did your cell phone salesperson present even ten percent of the functions that are standard on your new phone? Chances are that you and your client have never seen a perfect product presentation. This leads to a major question: How can we give a perfect value presentation if we have never seen one?

> *In today's internet shopping market, the only way a client will stop shopping and purchase is when they are confident there is no more information available that they would know how to ask to find.*

In other words, you presented the product better than what they feel they could find on their own. You have now become your client's teacher, advisor, consultant and expert. When this occurs, Value exceeds Cost and your client will purchase!

One challenge you will face is when your competition only builds half of the Value and leaves your client wanting to buy for half the Cost. Take solace in knowing that if your competition did everything correctly, the client would not be in front of you. If you are the first salesperson to build the correct Value, you will make the sale. You can rest assured that if your Value greatly exceeds your Cost, your client will feel confident enough to make a purchase now.

Putting The Scale of the Sale Principle to Work

The following questions are designed to gain a working understanding and real application in your business and in your life. Always try to answer the following questions before moving on to the next principle. This will provide you the opportunity to reflect on the value of each principle as a standalone concept. The more quality effort you apply to your answers, the better chance you will see immediate and lasting results from the value of each principle. The questions below are the same at the end of each chapter. Being cognizant of this will allow you to develop an action plan for putting the principles to work as you continue to read.

Define the key points of this principle that you will apply in your business.

Give an example of how the author demonstrated the principle.

Write three real examples of what you would say to your clients to show how you can apply this principle in your business.

Define three plans to exemplify ways that this principle will increase the quality of your selling process, margins, volume, and relationship with your clients.

Write an analogy of how this principle would apply outside of business.

43

FIVE

Allow The Purchasing Decision to be Your Client's

Not so long ago, when your clients first started considering purchasing your product, there was a process they had to go through. First, they would see the product on TV, or a neighbor or coworker was using one or talking positively about the product. Then came the justification, "I deserve it, I can afford it, I will use it, and best of all, this product will improve my life." After exposure and justification, your client started the research and shopping step. This used to be done by going to multiple businesses over a period of days, months, and sometimes years.

Good news! The internet, while it may not have helped to speed up the deliberate buyer, for everyone else it has cut shopping time drastically. Today, when a client comes into your business, they have already shopped, researched, and determined that your business is the place to go. They have dreamed, justified, and done all the research they need to empower themselves to come to your business. The only remaining factors are physically touching the product, and having enough confidence through education to make a purchasing decision.

Since it is your client's decision to come to your business, your job is to continue to support and educate them on what they already believe is correct. When your client finishes your sentences, or answers your questions before the whole question is asked, it is good! One example of this is an old word track that may apply to your business. It would be how we ask a client if they wish to pay cash or finance. If we are simply trying to get the answer the old way: "How were you wanting to handle the balance today, pay cash or finance?" This old way sounds like we are asking the question to get what we need to make a sale.

If we are to allow the purchasing decision to be our customer's, a better way to ask the same question would go as follows: "Were you thinking you wanted to be like most of our clients and make payments, or (pause and let the client answer)?" If the client interrupts and says they are paying cash, you could continue by saying: "Now is that going to be write a check type of cash or (pause and let the client tell you if it is real cash, or they have a preset loan from their own financial institution)?" You can confirm after they say write a check by saying, "So no preset loans?"

If the example above is tough to follow because it is out of context, the main point is to let the client manage you in helping them purchase. Remember, it was their idea to come here to see the product that they have already researched and have an intent to purchase. Over the years I have heard a lot of top salespeople say, "Sometimes I just need to get out of the way of a client who wants to buy my product." Don't feel like you need to say everything that you have learned in sales training courses to every client. Say only what you need, to help the client accomplish their goal in coming into your business today.

While this final statement appears in other principles, it is worth mentioning now: It is not your job to sell your product, it is your job to help your client purchase. Try to move beyond this statement and focus on your client using the product, not the buying and selling process. Help your client see themselves using and enjoying the product years into the future.

Putting The Allow The Purchasing Decision to be Your Client's Principle to Work

The following questions are designed to gain a working understanding and real application in your business and in your life. Always try to answer the following questions before moving on to the next principle. This will provide you the opportunity to reflect on the value of each principle as a standalone concept. The more quality effort you apply to your answers, the better chance you will see immediate and lasting results from the value of each principle. The questions below are the same at the end of each chapter. Being cognizant of this will allow you to develop an action plan for putting the principles to work as you continue to read.

Define the key points of this principle that you will apply in your business.

Give an example of how the author demonstrated the principle.

Write three real examples of what you would say to your clients to show how you can apply this principle in your business.

Define three plans to exemplify ways that this principle will increase the quality of your selling process, margins, volume, and relationship with your clients.

Write an analogy of how this principle would apply outside of business.

SIX

THE CIRCLE AND SQUARE

In a statistics course, a professor drew several straight lines on a board and asked students to come up before the class and draw a mark where the center of the line should be without use of measuring instruments. Then, with proper measuring tools, the professor was able to prove that the human eye is remarkably accurate. The reason we use a circle and a square to line up a client's budget with a product is the same. While it may be impossible to have exactly the perfect product in inventory that also matches the client's budget 100% of the time, it is possible to be close, sometimes very close.

Before explaining the solution, let's look at where the need for this principle started. Picture a client coming into your business and falling in love with a product which, hours later, they find that they can't afford. While this can seem unlikely, many sales managers in many industries are trained to tell their salespeople, "Don't worry about the money, just go make them love the product. If they love the product, we can put it together at the end. We have negotiation skills that we can use to get them to pay more at the end of the selling process."

Wow! Can you even imagine that this type of sales still exists? When this happens, the salesperson comes back to the manager two hours later, has made the client fall in love with a product that will cost $800 per month, and has just found out that their budget is only $400 per month. Ironically, the same sales manager who two hours before said, "Don't worry about the money," is now screaming at the salesperson, "You idiot, you landed them on too much product!" Let's follow the above manager's statements to their three illogical conclusions when the client has fallen in love with a product (the Square) that is much larger than their budget (the Circle).

Option One: When the square is much larger than the circle, the salesperson is often sent out by the manager to bump the client. This means that the salesperson is expected to get the client to spend more than their budget. This makes the client feel uncomfortable, and should make the salesperson and manager feel the same way. The problem with these old sales tactics is even if you get the client to spend more, they will never refer a friend to receive the same stressful service. Beating up and bullying your clients is no way to build a business. If you ever see a salesperson with no repeat and referral business, you should never copy their tactics.

Option Two: When the square is much larger than the circle, you could give up profit to make up for your client not having enough money to pay for the product with which you made them fall in love. This option violates a universal truth in sales: The clients who pay the most profit are always the most satisfied. This is also a self-fulfilling prophecy. When a client pays the profit that is suggested by the manufacturer (MSRP), the business has the reserve to give outstanding service after the sale. When the profit is compromised, so is the service; there is no money available to provide the service the client will be expecting. Your clients expect that you will make enough to be there for them when they need you.

Option Three: Last, when the square is much larger than the circle, you may think of switching your clients to a smaller square that fits their small circle. The problem with this option is that after you spend at least two hours making your client love a product, and then try to switch them to a lesser product, you may turn them into shoppers. They can leave and try to find the same larger square that you made them fall in love with at a different business (not yours) for less money. When they find after shopping that it is not possible, a second universal truth will apply: Your clients always buy from the last place they shop. Trying to switch your clients is disrespectful and is not necessary if you had lined up The Circle and Square correctly prior to showing the wrong product that doesn't fit your client's budget.

There are many mothers who have told their daughters that it is just as easy to fall in love with a rich man as a poor man, but if you never date a rich man, how will you know? Putting this in sales language: It is just as easy to fall in love with a product you can afford as one you can't afford, but if no one ever shows you the one you can afford, how will you know?

This principle is about taking the time in a product selection step, prior to showing a product, to make sure that you show the right product that fits your client's wants, needs, and budget. You know that you are executing this principle when you get to the end of your selling process and there is no stress, no negotiations (because you are under your client's budget), and finally your client is so pleased that they can't wait to send you referrals.

Putting The Circle and Square Principle to Work

The following questions are designed to gain a working understanding and real application in your business and in your life. Always try to answer the following questions before moving on to the next principle. This will provide you the opportunity to reflect on the value of each principle as a standalone concept. The more quality effort you apply to your answers, the better chance you will see immediate and lasting results from the value of each principle. The questions below are the same at the end of each chapter. Being cognizant of this will allow you to develop an action plan for putting the principles to work as you continue to read.

Define the key points of this principle that you will apply in your business.

Give an example of how the author demonstrated the principle.

Write three real examples of what you would say to your clients to show how you can apply this principle in your business.

Define three plans to exemplify ways that this principle will increase the quality of your selling process, margins, volume, and relationship with your clients.

Write an analogy of how this principle would apply outside of business.

SEVEN

WE CARE

This principle, while the title seems simple, can go as deep as the many definitions of the word care as a noun or a verb. As a noun, we are implying that we are prepared to provide a service. Caring also can mean that we wish to uphold a set standard in customer service. This principle works well as a noun.

As a verb it means to physically take a caring approach in our service to our clients. It can also take a cognitive action in how we think about our industry and providing for our client's needs. With a solid understanding of the title, let's break down this principle into three headings: We Care about our Clients; We Care about our Business; We Care about our Industry.

First, caring about our clients, has two parts. Part one implies that we genuinely care about the well-being of our clients. Take business out of this for a second, and ask yourself how you feel when a client is excited to show you their grandchild's picture. Do you just fake smile and want to get back to business? Do you feel like you have to be nice or the client will never buy from you? Do you feel like this could be ten minutes of your life that you will never get back? If you only see your clients as your next sale, the above questions may not only be how you feel, but could also be what you look like to others watching you pretend to be interested in something very important to your client.

The opposite of not caring is being genuinely there for your client. If your client took the time to show you their family pictures, they must value you as an extended family member. Instead of being put off by their actions, you should be honored that they wish to share something so personal with you. If you really care about your clients you will care all the time, not just when it is convenient.

The second part of caring about our clients is that our clients must know that we care about them. It is really hard to dislike someone who likes you. Take the time in your presentations to show appreciation and acknowledge your client's good ideas, useful facts they share and stories they tell. You will find that it is easy to care about your client when you look for the good in what they share with you.

The next part of this principle addresses the assertion We Care about our Business. A long time ago when our print business was just getting started we had a new employee who had made a mistake on the printing of a newsletter.

It was a large print job with a new client. The error was discovered while he was delivering the finished product to a client, located two hours away from our office, on a Friday. When I returned to the office late on that same Friday, he was just leaving to deliver the fixed product for the second time, and it was then after 5:00. I didn't know there was an error, I just assumed that he finished late and was making a delivery deadline. After he left I noticed all of the original flawed product in the office. On Monday I learned that he paid for the new paper out of his own pocket and didn't expense his second set of delivery miles. This is a person who cares about the business.

I would like to believe that all employees care about the success of their business, but in that same business, we had another publisher who would waste paper, ink, toner, take long lunches and breaks. She would rarely be to work on time and never stay late to take care of a client. Then something happened. She reached her vesting period where she started earning profit sharing. Suddenly paper clips were being reused, we printed on both sides of paper and she even brought in a coffee mug so that the company didn't have to keep buying cups. It was too bad that she didn't see all along that the company was providing her with a good living and a career opportunity. The health of your business is directly related to the good work you put forth on a daily basis. If you care about your business, your business will be there to take care of you.

One other consideration in caring for your business is recognizing that you are an ambassador carrying your business flag. This means that if you are wearing company logo-wear, everywhere you go everyone knows where you work. In public you and your company are judged by your behavior. If you threw chairs on the basketball court while coaching, you and your employer are judged by your behavior. As a salesperson, you will meet many clients who buy and who will never buy, but your odds of running into both at the local grocery store are the same.

Finally, this principle states: We Care about our Industry. As a sales training company, many times we find ourselves doing business with several competitors in the same city. I was shocked the first time I heard a client say that if they don't make the sale, they don't want their competition to make the sale either. This doesn't make sense. If we sell boats, and we don't make the sale and also mess up the sale for everyone else selling boats, that client may buy a hot tub.

Now, instead of that client saying to all their friends we bought a boat and you should too, they're telling their friends to buy a hot tub. If all the boat salespeople feel the same in that town, the boat business will be gone shortly. If your client does not buy from you, you want them to buy in your same industry even if it is from a competitor. We, as salespeople, are responsible for protecting our industry.

While training in Canada at an RV business, I observed a frustrated client and listened to his story. He said he was very excited to purchase his motorhome and travel down to the states. While he was on holiday in the states his RV broke down. He went to several places and no one would fix his problem. They said they were too busy or only worked on their own client's RVs. The client was giving the keys back to the Canadian dealer and said that he didn't want the RV anymore because he could not get it serviced. The industry lost that client, and possibly everyone he speaks to for the rest of his life.

To be effective at executing the We Care Principle we must have empathy for everyone all the time. We must care for our clients and be sure that they know that we care. We must care for our business to guarantee its survival to be there to take care of our clients' future needs. Lastly, we must care and protect our industry by taking care of all of our industry's clients.

Putting The We Care Principle to Work

The following questions are designed to gain a working understanding and real application in your business and in your life. Always try to answer the following questions before moving on to the next principle. This will provide you the opportunity to reflect on the value of each principle as a standalone concept. The more quality effort you apply to your answers, the better chance you will see immediate and lasting results from the value of each principle. The questions below are the same at the end of each chapter. Being cognizant of this will allow you to develop an action plan for putting the principles to work as you continue to read.

Define the key points of this principle that you will apply in your business.

Give an example of how the author demonstrated the principle.

Write three real examples of what you would say to your clients to show how you can apply this principle in your business.

Define three plans to exemplify ways that this principle will increase the quality of your selling process, margins, volume, and relationship with your clients.

Write an analogy of how this principle would apply outside of business.

EIGHT

ANCHORING

8

The way you ask a question greatly influences the answer.

Picture this: You are casually walking down the street when a stranger walks up and asks, "The Mississippi River is 500 miles long: True or false?" How would you answer? In a study of 10,000 random people, the answers ranged from true (500 miles) to guesses up to 1,500 miles. Another 10,000 people were presented with a different question. They were asked, "The Mississippi River starts at the top of Minnesota and meanders until it finally pours into the Gulf of Mexico. With all that distance and meandering, the Mississippi River is 5,000 miles long; True or false?" This time the answers ranged from as low as 3,500 to the 5,000 miles that was suggested in the question. The control in this study or the constant was that the Mississippi River did not change its course throughout this study. This illustrates the concept of Anchoring. The story above is supported by the 2007 study conducted by the Department of Psychology at Appalachian State University on the Anchoring Effect[2].

2   Dowd, Keith, and Todd McElroy. "Susceptibility to Anchoring Effects: How Openness-to-experience Influences Responses to Anchoring Cues." *Judgment and Decision Making* 2.1 (2007): 48-53. Web. 09 Sept. 2014. <http://journal.sjdm.org/jdm06143.pdf>.

Anchoring:
The way we ask questions
greatly influences the answers.

To better serve our customers, we must use anchors throughout our sales presentations. In a well delivered presentation, you will find anchors are used to relax defensive customers, discover shopping budgets, find out if a customer has a trade, sell from stock, explain why some products cost more, increase down payments, negotiate at the write-up, set appointments, handle service heat and most important of all, protect your client's right to purchase the best product their money can buy. When used correctly, Anchoring is so powerful that it can even keep a client from concealing the truth. This allows you to give the best service that all of your clients deserve.

Our clients' dishonesty may come from mistrust triggered by a poor experience at another business, or that they may just be outside of their comfort zone. Either way, we must ask quality questions, early and often, to help our clients give us accurate information so that we may provide them with better service.

To make this point clearly, we can analyze the questions commonly asked by salespeople in the product selection step that follows:

A. What would you like your payments to be?

Not Productive Anchoring! There are too many possible answers, such as: What do you think my payments would be on this product? As low as possible! The same as my last product! We want our payments to be $250 per month. As a result of the question's wording, the salesperson has limited choices of presentable products. The customer may never really have the opportunity to purchase what they can really afford!

B. What are your current monthly payments?

Not Productive Anchoring! This question is irrelevant, makes no sense, and is in fact the perfect example of a negative or reverse anchor. The customer is probably wishing to purchase a product that costs more money than their trade-in, they may have very little for a down payment, and finally, they could owe more on their trade than it is worth. Therefore, it is impossible to keep their same monthly payments. Why lead the customer to believe this can be done?

C. So I don't waste your time showing you the wrong product, as far as your monthly payments, where did you want to start looking $500 - $550 per month, $550-$600, $700, $800, $1,000 per month?

This is Productive Anchoring! The customer will probably stop you long before you get to the top range. Expect an answer like: "Whoa! I can only afford $400 per month!" You have now effectively discovered the customer's budget and can be truly principle centered, showing them only what they can afford.

With Anchoring, you can expect the customer to select the lowest number that leaves your mouth or their budget - whichever value is lower!

This principle focuses on the importance of increasing the quality of communication between a salesperson and their customer. Anchoring may be the single most effective way to increase your gross profit, your volume, and your customer service all at the same time!

Putting The Anchoring Principle to Work

The following questions are designed to gain a working understanding and real application in your business and in your life. Always try to answer the following questions before moving on to the next principle. This will provide you the opportunity to reflect on the value of each principle as a standalone concept. The more quality effort you apply to your answers, the better chance you will see immediate and lasting results from the value of each principle. The questions below are the same at the end of each chapter. Being cognizant of this will allow you to develop an action plan for putting the principles to work as you continue to read.

Define the key points of this principle that you will apply in your business.

Give an example of how the author demonstrated the principle.

Write three real examples of what you would say to your clients to show how you can apply this principle in your business.

Define three plans to exemplify ways that this principle will increase the quality of your selling process, margins, volume, and relationship with your clients.

Write an analogy of how this principle would apply outside of business.

NINE

TIME FRAME △▽

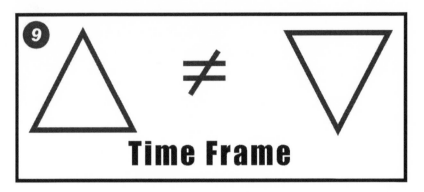

Ask yourself: Twenty years ago, how many of your buyers in their 60's owned computers and were comfortable using them to research their purchases? Conversely, how many of today's 60 year olds (who were 40 years old twenty years ago) use computers to be highly informed buyers? The consumer's education level has increased drastically in the last twenty years. If you have not updated your selling style and technique, you are guaranteed to be left behind. This principle outlines a good first step to modernizing your sales presentation.

The triangles pictured above represent the Time Frame of the selling process. The triangle on the left represents what has been handed down over the years as the proper time frame of the sale. It represents very little time at the "Meet and Greet" step and a long drawn out "Closing" step. The "Closing" step takes so long because the salesperson is often trying to grind money from the client that they do not know if they have or don't have. For example, an offer would be put in front of a manager where the customer wants to spend $400 per month on a product that will actually cost $800 per month. This offer that does not fit the client's budget sets you up for a long negotiation. This old style of sales (Time Frame) is disrespectful to the customer and demoralizing to the salesperson. Dealers who have not experienced significantly less floor traffic while still experiencing a decline in sales can partially credit this to their lack of growth.

The triangle on the right represents a time frame that is much more consistent with the way consumers prefer to shop and buy today. Spending more time listening to the wants, needs, and budget of our client is critical. Remember that they have more information today than ever before. Allowing the customer to present their own research is respectful, allows us to show them what they want, and most importantly, what fits their budget! When this is done correctly, your closing will come fast and with very little negotiations. The stress for both the client and salesperson will disappear.

Recently a new salesperson was explaining that the left triangle is the old wrong way, and the one on the right was the new and correct way of managing service time to their client. The salesperson was asked if they ever sold using the left triangle time frame. When they answered, "No" it came to their attention that the old way has never applied to them and never will. Today's sales professionals have an advantage. They do not have to unlearn bad habits. People who are new to sales have the advantage of still thinking like a consumer. A modern consumer. Today they enter a sales career without having to handle objections from the past that are no longer relevant.

The best way to sum up this principle is to sell the way your clients want to buy. Take your time at the beginning. Get to know and enjoy your clients' stories about how they will use your product. Learn why they want to purchase, and what brought them to you. At the end, you will be in a position to allow your client to spend what they told you earlier with no stress. This makes the time frame at the bottom of the triangle on the right so fast.

Putting The Time Frame
Principle to Work

The following questions are designed to gain a working understanding and real application in your business and in your life. Always try to answer the following questions before moving on to the next principle. This will provide you the opportunity to reflect on the value of each principle as a standalone concept. The more quality effort you apply to your answers, the better chance you will see immediate and lasting results from the value of each principle. The questions below are the same at the end of each chapter. Being cognizant of this will allow you to develop an action plan for putting the principles to work as you continue to read.

Define the key points of this principle that you will apply in your business.

Give an example of how the author demonstrated the principle.

Write three real examples of what you would say to your clients to show how you can apply this principle in your business.

Define three plans to exemplify ways that this principle will increase the quality of your selling process, margins, volume, and relationship with your clients.

Write an analogy of how this principle would apply outside of business.

TEN

INTERACTIVE PRESENTATION

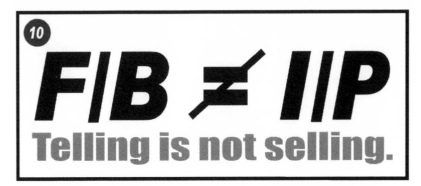

As a follow-up to the Time Frame Principle, there are new sales techniques that must be implemented. With the undesirable triangle Time Frame, most of the sales efforts come at the end where salespeople are trying to scramble to build value to compensate for the cost of the product.

To transition to the effective triangle Time Frame, where there is no need for negotiation at the end of the selling process, we must first replace Feature/Benefit selling in the product presentation step with Interactive Presentations.

The Interactive Presentation is about really listening in the product selection (interview/qualify) step and building a presentation to fit the needs of the client. Once the needs of the client are identified, it becomes easy to create or identify a problem in the customer's life and solve it with a feature on the product you are presenting. Remember this is an Interactive Presentation which means that the client should be doing most of the talking. You simply create the problem, pause, and let the client run with how the problem relates to them. After they tell you about their experience with that problem, you explain how the feature works, and let the customer realize they must have that feature that solves their needs. Some light examples are below.

PROBLEM
  → *SOLVE PROBLEM (FEATURE)*
Slipping on wet steps
  → Non-skid steps

Having to stop quickly at highway speeds
  → Anti-lock brakes

Breaking down fishing poles to secure them at night
  → Limited storage space

Having the door open with no bugs
  → Screen door

Sunburn, shade and rain protection
  → Awning

No transportation with a wrecked car
  → Rental Insurance Coverage

Once the features are sold correctly, we load them into a shopping cart and are ready to start scanning them for money.

As the following is an example of a summary close, try to see how this justifies features for value the same way a clerk at the grocery store would scan each item before asking for money. Last, before you try this closing technique, be sure to write at least fifteen features on your write-up sheet that are important to the customer from the Interactive Presentation that you can point to during the close.

SUMMARY CLOSE EXAMPLE FOR AN R.V. WHILE PRESENTING A MONTHLY PAYMENT TO YOUR CUSTOMER:

"Your monthly payment is $550 and it looks like you are getting everything you wanted with the (point to your list of features on that same page) air conditioning, because you said you would be doing most of your camping in the summer; with the non-skid steps, so you do not have to worry about slipping going out for your morning walks; and the island queen bed, because you both said you hated making the corner bed or sleeping against the wall. It sounds like we are going the right direction - - you seem to have what you want and the monthly payment fits the budget you outlined for me earlier so - - just put your OK here x____."

As you should conclude from reading the above example, there are many other steps in your "Road to the Sale" that must be executed properly before attempting this technique. Most important would be how and where in advance your clients told you that they wanted $550 per month for a payment (for the answer reference back to The Circle and Square Principle).

As with any new technique, the more often you use Interactive Presentations and Value-Based Closing, the more comfortable you will become. Once you start justifying the value of what you are selling you will see more full-price purchases with more satisfied clients! Conversely, you can expect that the next time you catch yourself using the old "If I Could, Would You" approach and the customer says, "NO," you will become angry with yourself as your only next move is to go down in price or start giving away extras!

Putting The Interactive Presentation Principle to Work

The following questions are designed to gain a working understanding and real application in your business and in your life. Always try to answer the following questions before moving on to the next principle. This will provide you the opportunity to reflect on the value of each principle as a standalone concept. The more quality effort you apply to your answers, the better chance you will see immediate and lasting results from the value of each principle. The questions below are the same at the end of each chapter. Being cognizant of this will allow you to develop an action plan for putting the principles to work as you continue to read.

Define the key points of this principle that you will apply in your business.

Give an example of how the author demonstrated the principle.

Write three real examples of what you would say to your clients to show how you can apply this principle in your business.

Define three plans to exemplify ways that this principle will increase the quality of your selling process, margins, volume, and relationship with your clients.

Write an analogy of how this principle would apply outside of business.

ELEVEN

ONLY SPEAK WHEN

**Don't speak unless it is in direct
benefit to your client.**

This principle, while unbelievably easy to present and comprehend, is one of the most challenging to execute day in and day out. The complete title of this principle goes as follows: We are not allowed to open our mouth unless what we are saying is in direct benefit to our clients.

Fighting our natural tendencies to share our personal experiences with a newfound friend (our client) is challenging to say the least. For example you may just be at the meet and greet step in your selling process and notice your client is wearing a pair of Keen brand shoes. Knowing full well that your goal in this first step in your selling process is to find a safe place to communicate, you go off talking about the Keen shoes that you just bought. You may fill the next ten minutes talking about why you purchased the shoes, what you paid, what you use them for, all while boring your client to sleep. They didn't come to your business to listen to what you think about their shoes, they came for your expertise on the product they are interested in purchasing for their own use.

What makes this principle so difficult is that we in the sales industry inherently enjoy people and sharing our experiences with anyone who will listen. When a client tells you they love to fish, ask them about their experiences. Where they go, what bait they use, what time of year and what type of fishing they enjoy? At no time should you share your fishing stories. This is your client's time and their billable hours.

Think as if you are paid
by the hour by your client,
and they are paying you to listen
to their wants, needs, and budget
for the product they wish to purchase.

Many salespeople feel that if they share their personal experiences in life it will make them seem more human and approachable. While there is some truth to this, make your stories short, and move the examples back to your client's experiences as soon as possible. If your client asks personal questions, for example: "How many kids do you have?" Give them a direct answer and then ask the same question of them. Continue to ask more about their family and let the day be totally about your client.

As caring people we enjoy sharing our successes and life challenges with our clients. Since many of our clients we see more than even our close friends and family members, we may start believing that our clients see us the same way. We must, however, remember to keep business, business. Over the years you will develop many true friendships with your clients. The time to share is when you are away from the business setting and off the clock. A word of caution however: Are you ever really off the clock? Anything you say or do will be remembered when you get back to the workplace. There may be some things you say that you will never be able to recover from. If you have to question whether you should say something, the safest bet will always be: Don't open your mouth unless what you are saying is in direct benefit to your client!

Putting The Only Speak
When Principle to Work

The following questions are designed to gain a working understanding and real application in your business and in your life. Always try to answer the following questions before moving on to the next principle. This will provide you the opportunity to reflect on the value of each principle as a standalone concept. The more quality effort you apply to your answers, the better chance you will see immediate and lasting results from the value of each principle. The questions below are the same at the end of each chapter. Being cognizant of this will allow you to develop an action plan for putting the principles to work as you continue to read.

Define the key points of this principle that you will apply in your business.

Give an example of how the author demonstrated the principle.

Write three real examples of what you would say to your clients to show how you can apply this principle in your business.

Define three plans to exemplify ways that this principle will increase the quality of your selling process, margins, volume, and relationship with your clients.

Write an analogy of how this principle would apply outside of business.

TWELVE

DOWNSTREAM SELLING

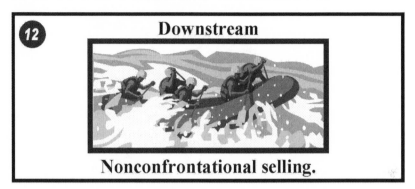

⑫ **Downstream**

Nonconfrontational selling.

Another term that is commonly used synonymously with Downstream Selling is nonconfrontational selling. As you read this chapter, ask yourself if nonconfrontational selling is a style or a life choice? With this principle, the very title suggests that there may be no place in the entire selling process for a fight. If you like conflict, selling may be a challenging career choice. There are many times where you can think you are correct and chose to defend your ideals and beliefs; only later you realize that it is your clients who are spending the money and should get what they want!

As this principle is examined, it is imperative that we recognize the relative link between Downstream Selling and many of the other principles in this book. For example, The Graph Principle that explains the importance of building a client base could never be realized. To be able to do any sort of follow-up, where the client will take your call, listen to a message, or even read a follow-up letter, the salesperson's presentation must be professional, modern and above all, without conflict. The modern salesperson does not use clichéd lines like, "If I Could, Would You?" nor do they use old techniques like feature/benefit presentations. How our customers purchase is changing daily. As you read on, ask yourself if you are employing a selling technique and using a style, or do you really believe that truthful nonconfrontational selling will benefit your customers and business now and for the future.

Understanding Downstream Selling is the first step to becoming nonconfrontational. The best way to explain Downstream Selling is with a quick story. "Picture yourself on a boat on a river with tangerine trees and marmalade skies"[3] (if you are a Beatles fan, you get it). As peaceful as this may sound, your whitewater adventure begins as you turn the bend. Now you find yourself in Class IV rapids, holding on to the boat and your paddle, and listening to your guide shout instructions to navigate the current. After you survive the rapids, the most deadly part of the rafting trip awaits.

The water calms, and you look ahead to see that you are heading toward a waterfall. This is not a wimpy waterfall; you must get to shore quickly or you will not survive. The guide in the back of the boat once again shouts a command, "Full paddle." While you fight the urge to look back at him to see if he is crazy, you follow his instructions again because you want to live! Once you are halfway through the first stroke you notice the boat is calmly and safely gliding to shore. Your guide simply needed the boat to be moving faster than the

3   The Beatles. *Lucy in the Sky with Diamonds.* George Martin, 1967. Vinyl recording

current to allow his rudder to work and get you out of harm's way.

Downstream Selling works the same way. For example, you are walking out to show your first product and your customer asks, "What are you going to give me for my trade?" First you must jump in the boat with your customer, paddle the same direction and then apply the rudder and steer with no conflict. Your response could be, "If you are like most of our customers, you are going to want maximum allowable for your trade? So what if my manager gives you two, three or even five thousand more for your trade than you were even expecting and we still can't find a product you would like to own - - will it matter what he gives you for your trade if there is no product you like? Let's start looking at products, and if you find one you like, at that point I will remind my manager that you are going to demand maximum allowable for your trade." There is no conflict as you proceed to show your first model.

Another example would be if your client wants to make an issue over your interest rate while you are discussing monthly payments on the product they are trying to purchase. The Downstream Selling technique would sound like this: "What if we could get you a 1, 2, or even 3 percent lower interest rate than you were even expecting and we still couldn't get the payments to fit with the rest of your monthly bills, would it matter? What if we make sure there is a payment that will work in your budget, and then fill out a credit application and submit your loan application to the bank? Without the product fitting your budget, the rest will not matter."

This chapter could be filled easily with example after example of Downstream Selling; however there is a much larger question that must be addressed. Do you believe in what you do for a living? If you do not look at the whole picture Downstream Selling is just a technique to get you to the next step and eventually close a deal. While it comes off as smooth, this powerful technique is tied closely to the other selling principles. Without nonconfrontational selling many of the other principles would have no glue to hold them together.

THE FOLLOWING PRINCIPLES WOULD BE INEFFECTIVE IF THERE WAS CONFLICT IN YOUR SALES PRESENTATION:

The Graph: With conflict you get no repeat or referral business.

Selling by Compartments: With conflict you will appear to be closing all the time.

Get Permission First: With conflict you come off as trying to do something to the customer and not for the customer.

Interactive Presentations: With conflict you may find yourself actually arguing with a customer about what features are best for them.

Value-Based Summary Close: With conflict you often find yourself telling rather than selling.

Anchoring: With conflict you never really listen to the customer's needs because you never ask the right questions.

Triangle Time Frame of Sale: With conflict it is easy to become unorganized with your presentation as it relates to the next step. The triangle could flip leaving you with an unhealthy grind to close the sale. No one leaves happy!

Tying the principles together must be a life choice, not just a style. If this is truly your career, and not just a job, you must be the best in the industry! Your clients, spending their hard-earned money, expect a professional with a long-term commitment to product knowledge, selling skills, follow-up, integrity, honesty and trust. It is not easy to help customers purchase your products; it requires hard work and dedication to your trade.

The rewards are great! Sales is a profession where the average income can be two to four times higher than what the average income is in your county, state or province. This is also a career where you get to help people get what they want, and that often means improving the quality of their lives. There are not too many opportunities left where you get to help customers and get paid well for your efforts.

The last point that must be addressed is, when do you never use Downstream Selling? Truly, never use Downstream Selling when you are closing the sale or asking for the order. The definition of closing goes as follows: When the answer confirms a sale. When you ask for the order correctly, the answer can only be yes or no. Downstream Selling could get in the way if you said with no conflict, "You could buy if you wanted?" The closing techniques that are most effective summarize the value that is perceived by your client and offer a logical conclusion. Let your clients purchase what they want and came in to buy.

Putting The Downstream Selling Principle to Work

The following questions are designed to gain a working understanding and real application in your business and in your life. Always try to answer the following questions before moving on to the next principle. This will provide you the opportunity to reflect on the value of each principle as a standalone concept. The more quality effort you apply to your answers, the better chance you will see immediate and lasting results from the value of each principle. The questions below are the same at the end of each chapter. Being cognizant of this will allow you to develop an action plan for putting the principles to work as you continue to read.

Define the key points of this principle that you will apply in your business.

Give an example of how the author demonstrated the principle.

Write three real examples of what you would say to your clients to show how you can apply this principle in your business.

Define three plans to exemplify ways that this principle will increase the quality of your selling process, margins, volume, and relationship with your clients.

Write an analogy of how this principle would apply outside of business.

83

THIRTEEN

"If I Could, Would You?" Is Not a Value-Based Summary Close

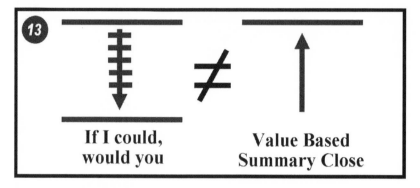

To embrace this principle a paradigm shift may be in order. Starting with the old, "If I could sell you this product for this price will you buy today?" This old sales tactic will not work effectively in today's competitive market where margins are already cut and little room is left for discounting. This old style teaches that salespeople should start high to leave room for negotiation. With the internet blasting low prices from businesses, even out of your market, if your prices are too high to start with your phone may never ring, and your front door may never swing. Also, clients are taught to start their offers low to combat these old tactics. If they start low and you start lowering your price from the inflated price, the client will just keep saying no and watch you keep coming down in your price.

Imagine you are at the local grocery store, and just like always, you push your cart up to the check-out line when the clerk says, "I'm in a big hurry, I have to pick up my wife and kids and get to the ballgame. My line is nine customers deep and I'm off in ten minutes. Can I check you out the quick way; I'll save you time and money?" Recognizing that the clerk has been there ten-plus years and wanting to be polite, you say sure (in a questioning tone). The clerk puts his hands around your cart sizing it up (without touching one item) and says, "That will be $154.27, would you like paper or plastic?" At this point you may look at him like he is crazy and say, "NO!" The clerk's quick reply would be, "What if I could drop the price to $150, would you buy today?" Of course you would still say, "NO!" The clerk's next move would be, "If I could drop the price to $140, throw in paper and plastic, would you buy today?" Of course, you would still say, NO! The clerk's next move would be, "If I could drop the price to $130 throw in paper, plastic, taxes and fees, would you buy today?" Still, NO! The more you say no, the more the clerk continues to drop the price. The clerk's next move may be, "If I could drop the price to $100, throw in paper, plastic, taxes, fees and free delivery would you buy today?" By now, along with thinking the clerk is crazy, you may have figured out that every time you say no the deal gets better. So you keep saying, "NO," and the clerk keeps saying, "If I could, would you?" and continuing to drop the price while throwing in more items!

If this type of behavior from a clerk sounds crazy in a grocery store, what does it sound like when you or your sales professionals employ the same tactics? The problem with these types of old outdated sales tactics are after spending five minutes discussing money with the clients, the clients forget what they are buying and it becomes all about the stress of spending their hard-earned money!

To better understand how to get to a productive solution to this problem we as an industry have created with old sales material, play some blackjack. Yes, the casino game of 21. Let's say the dealer has a down card and a queen as their up card. Understanding that there are 13 different cards in the deck and 4 of the 13 have a 10 value, you must believe that the dealer has a 20 (their down card is 4 times more likely to be worth 10 than any other card.) With you believing that the dealer has a 20 based on the queen you see, you look at your cards which are a 10 and a 2.

As you continue to look at the queen that has you beat on the table, you decide to take another card (a hit). You receive an ace! While you may think it is a good card, it is not so good for this hand. You look at the dealer's queen and think you need an eight. You know that you have an 8 in 13 chance that if you take another card it will help. You take the hit. You get another ace!

Now you have 14. You look at the dealer's queen believing they have a 20 and think that you need a 7. You know that you have a 7 in 13 chance that the next card will help (still better than 50%) and your $20 bet is already on the table. You take a hit. You get another ace!

Now you have 15 and this is where the gambling really starts. You know that you are beat on the table with the queen showing, but now you have a 6 in 13 chance that the next card will improve your hand. For the first time, if you take a hit, you will have less than a 50% chance that the card you receive will help your hand. You look at the queen and assume the dealer has a 20 with their down card and take a hit. You get another ace! At this point you have a 10, a 2, and 4 aces equaling 16.

The point of this blackjack game is to look at what motivated you to take four hits on your dealt hand of 12. Was it what you saw (the queen) or what you didn't see (the down card)? In blackjack, as in purchasing, you should always bet or buy what you see. You continued to take hits based on the presentation of the queen, not your guess of the down card. The proof is if the queen was a 6 next to the down card, you would never have hit once let alone four times. You would have presumed that the dealer still had a 10 down and let the dealer hit and hopefully bust.

So there is a good news/bad news to this blackjack story. The good news is that you have a queen to show your clients when you present your product. It is the value of the features you present to your client that they wish to own. Be sure to present your features well and when you ask for money, be sure to point out the value of your product just as the queen was the motivation for you to take another hit.

Now for the bad news. In blackjack the dealer's down card was never exposed. What if the dealer had a 6 as their down card? With the 6 and 10, equaling 16, the dealer would have had to take a hit, and most likely gone over 21 and busted. You, not knowing that they had a 6 down, could have busted four times before the dealer had a chance to lose. This happens in sales when clients are told not to worry about your prices and that you will give a large discount. The minute the client perceives that they will receive a large discount, they will expect it later.

Going back to the grocery store analogy will make more sense now. This time we will start the same way as before, but watch for the differences as the check-out clerk greets his client. "I'm in a big hurry, I have to pick up my wife and kids and get to the ballgame. My line is nine customers deep and I'm off in ten minutes. Can I check you out the quick way; I'll save you time and money?" Then the grocer proceeds to scan each of your items one at a time. You watch the register show the cost of each item as you hear a beeping sound from the scanner. Finally, your last item is scanned and you hear the grocer say, "Your total is $154.27, did you want paper or plastic?" Reflexively, you answer paper or plastic. The question posed to years of Sobel University students when presented with this scenario goes like this, "Why would the second grocery client pay full price, while the first client scenario wouldn't dream of it?" The answer has always been the same. The second client saw what they were getting for their money, the queen! You must show the client what they get for their hard-earned money when you ask for the order.

One final thought on the whole "If I Could, Would You" tactic. Since this is the most common close that your client may have heard from the last business that they didn't purchase from, if you say the same line, you could end up in the same place.

Putting The "If I Could, Would You?" Is Not a Value-Based Summary Close Principle to Work

The following questions are designed to gain a working understanding and real application in your business and in your life. Always try to answer the following questions before moving on to the next principle. This will provide you the opportunity to reflect on the value of each principle as a standalone concept. The more quality effort you apply to your answers, the better chance you will see immediate and lasting results from the value of each principle. The questions below are the same at the end of each chapter. Being cognizant of this will allow you to develop an action plan for putting the principles to work as you continue to read.

Define the key points of this principle that you will apply in your business.

Give an example of how the author demonstrated the principle.

Write three real examples of what you would say to your clients to show how you can apply this principle in your business.

Define three plans to exemplify ways that this principle will increase the quality of your selling process, margins, volume, and relationship with your clients.

Write an analogy of how this principle would apply outside of business.

FOURTEEN

BECAUSE OF OUR CLIENTS, WE EXIST!

> **14**
> # BECAUSE OF OUR CLIENTS WE EXIST.
> **We don't sell, we help people buy.**

If you are in the service industry, you are in sales! Whether you sell, install, teach, manage or invent, without your clients you wouldn't have a job. There was a young manager who actually posted a large sign on his door that read: Because Of Our Clients, We Exist! To make this an effective culture in his business, he had every person who entered his office read it out loud. This changed the way that the pursuing conversations unfolded. There was never a complaint about a client, ever! Everyone knew clearly that if they didn't have clients, they had no job.

The simplicity of this principle is critical to implementing a culture shift in your company. An analogy would be an American Lung Association's motto: "When you can't breathe, nothing else matters!" It's a simple statement that requires no explanation.

Once the culture of your business accepts this principle, you can move on to implementation. The next direction is to focus on what our clients need from us. Since our clients have thought about owning our products for some time, shopped online and possibly visited the competition, their goal is to own and use the product. Again, their goal is not to shop, not to buy, but to own and use the product. Thus, our goal is to help our clients purchase. Let's keep this principle this short and this sweet.

Putting The Because Of Our Clients, We Exist Principle to Work

The following questions are designed to gain a working understanding and real application in your business and in your life. Always try to answer the following questions before moving on to the next principle. This will provide you the opportunity to reflect on the value of each principle as a standalone concept. The more quality effort you apply to your answers, the better chance you will see immediate and lasting results from the value of each principle. The questions below are the same at the end of each chapter. Being cognizant of this will allow you to develop an action plan for putting the principles to work as you continue to read.

Define the key points of this principle that you will apply in your business.

Give an example of how the author demonstrated the principle.

Write three real examples of what you would say to your clients to show how you can apply this principle in your business.

Define three plans to exemplify ways that this principle will increase the quality of your selling process, margins, volume, and relationship with your clients.

Write an analogy of how this principle would apply outside of business.

FIFTEEN

HONESTY

15
Honesty

Never lie to your clients.
Never allow your clients to lie to you.

While shopping at a computer store a salesperson was asked about the compatibility of keypads from an old to new computer product. The salesperson replied that they were not compatible. The same salesperson was asked about docking stations and other accessories and told his client that none were available. The next day the client came back to return the keypad because his old one worked fine. The department manager said that the old one did work on the new product. After discovering that the store had all the accessories that the client wanted (that were supposedly not there the day before) the client made a large purchase, but was unhappy for the time wasted the day before.

The question before you is why do salespeople feel the need to not tell the truth, or just flat out lie? This could come from years of passed down training. For example, one manager defined three ways to lie and asked his salespeople which way is acceptable. He explained that the first way to lie is to outright not tell the truth. You know that the product coming in is blue and you tell the client that it is white. You make the sale on the order and plan to handle the heat later. You may even blame the color on your factory for sending the wrong one. In this case one lie leads to another.

He continued to explain that the second way to lie is to only tell the parts of the information that are true or correct. Justifying this behavior by saying that everything you say is truthful. Any way you look at this type of lying you have an intent to be deceptive.

The third type of lying is to tell the truth in a mocking or humorous tone. This way you are leading the client to not believe what you are saying and head the client away from the truth. Many salespeople believe this is alright because they never said anything but the truth.

So which of the above it the correct way to lie? Hopefully you said, "NONE OF THEM!" Professional salespeople have no need to lie. So what about the clients who lie? Have you heard the old saying, "Buyers are liars?" Many salespeople actually believe that since they are being lied to, it is alright to lie themselves.

Let's evaluate this "Buyers are liars" statement. Picture yourself at the dinner table with your spouse and talking about the new product you are going to purchase in the morning. You go to bed and dream of your new purchase. You wake up in the morning and put your feet on the floor and first thing out of your mouth in the morning is, "OK, today is the day I get to go lie to some salespeople." Of course, this is not what your client is thinking first thing in the morning after dreaming about your product. If anything, they are excited to get their new product and can't wait to use it.

So why do some clients lie? They didn't intend to when they woke up this morning. They have to know that if they lie, it could cost them the chance to get what they want. One reason they lie is because this is their defense against all the lying salespeople they have ever met in their life. Clients have a saying also, "You can tell if a salesperson is lying if their lips are moving." Did the sales industry earn this by believing that there are acceptable ways to lie? If you are in sales today are you expected to pay the price of every bad salesperson your client has ever met? By virtue of the fact that the client is in front of you, things must not have gone so well with the last salesperson.

This problem needs to be fixed. If no one trusts anyone, how can any client ever make a purchase and feel good about the experience. Justifying lying by saying you made the sale is not acceptable. You will harm your business, your industry and your ability to attract repeat and referrals. If you are a business owner, no good employees will want to work for or with you. They would be embarrassed to let family and friends be exposed to you as they know you would only say what you needed to earn favor.

The key to this principle is to never lie to a client. If you don't know the answer, simply say the truth, "I don't know the answer to your question. Let's find out together?" If you think you know but are not completely sure, you could say, "I have an answer to your question but I'm not sure it is the best answer. Since you deserve the best answer, let me think about this and if I need more information to get you the best answer, I will get it for you." Today's clients can check anything you say with their smartphone in seconds. If you get caught lying once, they will never trust anything you say in the future. It's not worth it! If you don't know the truth, get it for your client, and learn it for all your future clients.

Never lying to your clients is surprisingly easy and liberating. The hard part of this principle is to never allow your client to lie to you. What makes this so difficult is the client may lie to you so early in your selling process that even if you turn out to be the most honest reputable salesperson, they can't buy after they have lied. An example of this could be that the last salesperson's opening line to the client may have been, "Welcome to (their business name), my name is (they say their name) and yours is (they get your name)?" If this salesperson turns out to lie continuously, and you open with the same greeting, the client may lie about their name just to protect themselves. Later, even if the client wants to purchase from you, they would have to admit that they lied about their name.

When a client lies to you, take this very seriously. It means that you have not earned their trust. Ultimately, you will lose the sale and all future business from them and everyone they know. It could also mean that you remind them of someone else that they didn't like from the past. If you sense this, introduce the client to another salesperson from your business. Hopefully, they can still purchase from your business.

Unfortunately you will forever be paying the price for the poor treatment your client has received from all salespeople they have met up until now. The positive spin you have to accept is that the client is in front of you now. If in fact they received perfect service from the last salesperson, they would have purchased there. You now have the opportunity to show your client what a professional looks and sounds like. Make the best of it for yourself, your company, and for your industry. Remember, the truth is black and white. There is no gray area.

Putting The Honesty Principle to Work

The following questions are designed to gain a working understanding and real application in your business and in your life. Always try to answer the following questions before moving on to the next principle. This will provide you the opportunity to reflect on the value of each principle as a standalone concept. The more quality effort you apply to your answers, the better chance you will see immediate and lasting results from the value of each principle. The questions below are the same at the end of each chapter. Being cognizant of this will allow you to develop an action plan for putting the principles to work as you continue to read.

Define the key points of this principle that you will apply in your business.

Give an example of how the author demonstrated the principle.

Write three real examples of what you would say to your clients to show how you can apply this principle in your business.

Define three plans to exemplify ways that this principle will increase the quality of your selling process, margins, volume, and relationship with your clients.

Write an analogy of how this principle would apply outside of business.

SIXTEEN

GET PERMISSION FIRST

In the selling process, the word control has often referred to manipulation or getting to an advantageous position. Control, by this definition, has been made outdated by educated and empowered clients. Today's clients already know they want your product before they come to your business. There is no need to control or manipulate a client who already wants to own your product. This should change your selling process drastically. In Principle 14 we acknowledge that we do not sell, we help clients purchase. This principle shows how we do it, and offers an easy implementation strategy.

Since your clients already want your product, you just have to teach them how to buy. We have a selling process that is also a purchasing process. Depending on the complexity of your product, your clients need you to show them how to purchase. This involves explaining the steps to your client and getting permission to proceed in a step by step manner.

For example, if you are selling an RV you may say, "Rather than run the risk of showing you the wrong model, what if we sit down and you explain how you will use the RV? Will it be for long or short trips? Hot or cold climates? How many adults and kids will it need to sleep? What will you be towing it with, and where will you store the RV? This way we only show you what you want to see and not run the risk of wasting your time on the wrong product. How's that sound?" Your goal is to get permission to sit down with the client so they can help you help them.

Even as you present your product you can get permission to go clockwise around the product so that you are sure to cover every feature. "As we look at this product, what if we go clockwise around the product so we cover every feature? Not knowing what your favorites will be, we don't want to risk missing what could be very important to you." By agreeing with a direction in your presentation you will eliminate your client's stress by knowing what you will be doing next. This allows you to give a complete presentation and, as covered in other chapters, may very well be the best presentation your client has ever heard.

This principle suggests that you follow the next outlined steps. First, you suggest what you would like to do for the client next. Second, you get permission to proceed. Third, you do what you said you would and execute beyond your client's expectations. Fourth, you review to make sure you accomplished the client's goals in what you just covered. After you get confirmation that you are heading in the right direction, continue repeating the above steps until you have helped your clients purchase their new product.

If the last paragraph makes selling sound easy, that's because it is easy! Too often salespeople turn off their clients by pushing too hard. They think that they have to sell the product. The clients today do not need to be sold, rather they come to you for an education. Stop selling and just help your clients buy.

Putting The Get Permission
First Principle to Work

The following questions are designed to gain a working understanding and real application in your business and in your life. Always try to answer the following questions before moving on to the next principle. This will provide you the opportunity to reflect on the value of each principle as a standalone concept. The more quality effort you apply to your answers, the better chance you will see immediate and lasting results from the value of each principle. The questions below are the same at the end of each chapter. Being cognizant of this will allow you to develop an action plan for putting the principles to work as you continue to read.

Define the key points of this principle that you will apply in your business.

Give an example of how the author demonstrated the principle.

Write three real examples of what you would say to your clients to show how you can apply this principle in your business.

Define three plans to exemplify ways that this principle will increase the quality of your selling process, margins, volume, and relationship with your clients.

Write an analogy of how this principle would apply outside of business.

103

SEVENTEEN

INTEGRITY

Integrity

Protect your client, your dealer, your industry and your personal character.

To have Integrity means that one must adhere to moral and ethical principles. The question that gives salespeople a just or an unjust reputation focuses on the above word, adhere. While behavioral psychologists would argue whether the ability to follow a moral compass is innate or learned, it could be that salespeople just have not been trained properly and end up fabricating answers as situations present themselves. Today's salespeople must know the facts about their product or they will be exposed quickly by today's educated clients.

Then there is the other moral issue. What about the salesperson who has no moral compass and feels it is productive to say anything they need to say to close the sale? The cost of this salesperson is immeasurable. Many years ago a Chevrolet dealer brought Sobel University in to recruit and train for his newly purchased business. The consultant suggested that he hire the best available applicants based on education, ability to learn and quality of the applicant's character. It was suggested to the dealer that if he hires new people to the industry they would have no bad habits and would only perform by the way the dealer wanted to run his business.

This business owner told his consultant that he knew that the philosophy was correct. However, he expressed, with all of the other business owners in the area hiring new people to the industry, there must be many seasoned salespeople he could hire who would get him sales now. When the consultant explained that the reason these salespeople were available is because they did not produce at their last job, the dealer insisted he would hire them anyway. As a last attempt the consultant reminded the business owner that top salespeople do not walk away from their client base and a high paying job. Still the dealer did not budge from his beliefs; he wanted sales now!

As the consultant left, he told the business owner that he would be expecting a call in two to three years. The consultant knew that the dealer would damage his reputation so severely in that time that he would be calling for help once again.

Imagine that you just gave great service to your clients and they had to run to a PTA meeting. Before they left they made an appointment to come back to purchase at 10 am Saturday morning. While at the PTA meeting they shared with other parents how excited they were to get their new car on Saturday. Unfortunately, they were sharing their stories about the great service they received with another couple who had a very different experience at that same dealership. When the other couple spoke of the lying and deceptive practices that they experienced, the first couple had to regroup. In their conversation that ensued, "Were they just being nice to make the sale? What kind of a dealer would hire such a liar who is allowed to be deceptive? Why would they let him continue to work there if they know how he treats clients? If this is how they are before the sale, do I dare take my chances if I need help after I buy?"

Entire businesses are judged by the quality of their worst employee.

The answers to their questions made it impossible to show up for their Saturday appointment. The cost of an untrained or unethical salesperson to the dealership, and to the other sales professionals, is immeasurable.

Three years later the consultant answered the phone and it was the business owner calling right on time. The business owner expressed that his customer satisfaction index with the factory was the lowest in the region and that his reputation was so bad that no customers were coming into his business. Of course this was no surprise to the consultant since he knew that the dealer hired everyone else's nonproductive problem employees.

When the consultant met with the business owner this time, he appeared to be receptive when he asked what to do about his failing business. As the consultant knew the market (it was in the area he personally lived), he advised the business owner first to sell his business. The business owner answered quickly by saying, "That is not an option. I have been trying to sell it for one year already and no buyer wants to buy me out of my financial mess."

The next advice from the consult was to change the dealership name, or at least advertise - - "Under New Management." The business owner was also advised to change his staff and really be under new management. Unfortunately, once again, he chose not to follow the consultant's advice. He changed the name but none of the players. It's been said that the definition of insanity is doing the same thing over and over and expecting different results. That business owner went out of business and lost everything he had in the next six months.

Integrity in your business means that you believe that it is important to protect your client, your business owner, your industry, and your own personal character. A good example would be when a client comes into your business and expresses, "I'm buried!" You find this odd that these are the first words your client shares with you so you reply, "By saying you are buried, does this mean that you believe that you owe more on your trade than you think it is worth?" Without hesitation the client replies, "Yes."

To get to this point your client must have been to other businesses who told him that his situation was so grave that they couldn't help him. Maybe after hearing this over and over he picked up the new vernacular: buried, humpty, in the ditch, or even six feet under! The other business may have blamed the previous salesperson for selling a bad product, blamed the selling dealer for making too much profit, blamed the banks for charging too much interest on too long of a term, or even placed the blame on the manufacturer for their product not retaining its value. This is a perfect example of how not to demonstrate Integrity in your business or industry. If your client believes that the industry is bad, they will not purchase again, and they will be sure to tell their friends.

A properly trained salesperson would know just how to handle the situation above. They would say, "So when you say you are buried does that mean you believe you are in a reverse equity position with your trade?" After the client replies affirmatively, the salesperson would continue. "So for you to be in a reverse equity position it means that two great things must have occurred. First, you must have outstanding credit. The lenders only allow the clients with outstanding credit the opportunity to get extended terms so that during the loan period you could be in a reverse equity position. If you didn't have the good credit, the lenders would have structured your loan so that they would have always been in an equity position in case of default. Second, you must have purchased an outstanding product that the lenders knew would be of value even at the end of the term of the loan. So let me guess, when you purchased this product it fit your needs perfectly and now your needs have changed?" After another affirmative response, the salesperson would continue by saying, "Great, we can help you. If you still have that great credit, the lenders will let you be in a new reverse equity position. They just don't want to be in two reverse equity positions at one time. We can sit down and figure out what the banks will need to structure your new loan to get you the product that will fit your needs today."

In this response the new salesperson maintained Integrity by not putting down the trade product, the salesperson, the dealership, the industry, or even the manufacturer.

One last point on how Integrity is judged by our perception of reverse equity positions. It is unrealistic to believe that your clients will never be in a reverse equity position. If you went out to dinner last night and paid with your credit card, you are in a reverse equity position on your meal. You truly owe more on the meal than it is worth. If we could only buy what we could afford to buy with cash, the economy would shut down. As salespeople with Integrity we need to not judge our clients who just want our help, but rather we need to think and act as problem solvers.

Putting The Integrity Principle to Work

The following questions are designed to gain a working understanding and real application in your business and in your life. Always try to answer the following questions before moving on to the next principle. This will provide you the opportunity to reflect on the value of each principle as a standalone concept. The more quality effort you apply to your answers, the better chance you will see immediate and lasting results from the value of each principle. The questions below are the same at the end of each chapter. Being cognizant of this will allow you to develop an action plan for putting the principles to work as you continue to read.

Define the key points of this principle that you will apply in your business.

Give an example of how the author demonstrated the principle.

Write three real examples of what you would say to your clients to show how you can apply this principle in your business.

Define three plans to exemplify ways that this principle will increase the quality of your selling process, margins, volume, and relationship with your clients.

Write an analogy of how this principle would apply outside of business.

EIGHTEEN

PROTECT YOUR CLIENT'S RIGHT TO BUY FROM YOU TODAY

Protect your client's right to buy from you TODAY!

You have the best product knowledge, the best interactive presentation and the best service! NOW!

Picture a couple who has been dreaming about owning your product for days, weeks, months and sometimes even years. They have shopped businesses, gone to shows, talked to friends who own the same products, and even surfed the internet. The big day finally arrives when it is time to buy. They get up in the morning with a bounce in their step. The coffee tastes better and the air smells sweeter. This day starts out like a Broadway musical with a big opening song ("There's a bright yellow haze in the meadow ..." like in *Oklahoma*)[4]. You get the idea.

Then it's off to the merchant. Loaded with excitement your client has one objective, to buy so they can use their new toy.

---

4   *Oklahoma!* Dir. Fred Zinnemann. Perf. Gordon MacRae, Gloria Grahame, and Gene Nelson. Magna Theatre Corporation, 1955. Film.

What happens next could go either way. If the client ends up shopping at three places on their day off and doesn't get to buy, it is easy to identify how they feel by watching them as they leave your business at the end of the day. Their heads are down, they are taking small steps toward your exit and they have dejected looks on their faces. How could a day that started out with such promise have such an unfortunate ending?

To Protect Your Client's Right to Buy from You Today, you must bring three elements to the table. First, you must have the best product knowledge. The best simply means that you must be able to educate your client beyond what they can find themselves, and provide the knowledge that gives them the confidence to stop shopping and buy. If the client feels that there is no more they can learn by continuing to shop at other places as well as online, they will be ready to buy.

Second, you must deliver the best Interactive Presentation as explained in Principle 10. Explaining facts and figures does not make the presentation personalized to your client. The client needs to know that the product will satisfy their personal needs and not feel like you are just delivering the generic description on the cover of the box. Remember, telling is not selling. By identifying your client's needs and satisfying those needs the client will feel empowered to purchase.

Third, you must be ready to explain and deliver the best service after the sale. Many clients need to know why you are the best place to buy. Show your client your follow-up system. Introduce your clients to your service department. Show your clients your evidence manual with other clients' testimonials. Walk the client by your awards wall. And, maybe most important of all, look your clients in the eyes as you explain that this is your career and you plan on being here to take care of their future needs.

If you effectively accomplish all three of these objectives, your client will have the confidence to purchase right now. This means that if you are their first stop of the day and you handle all of your client's objectives beyond their expectations they will have no need to continue to shop. Christopher (Bo) Hurst, a very accomplished salesperson, at a Sobel University course insisted that the word NOW be added to this principle. Of course he was right on the mark. Understanding that as a commission salesperson, it is not acceptable that you just give the best service, you must get paid for that service. That's why you want to give the best and get paid now. Waiters who give the best service and don't receive their tip before the client leaves can pretty much count on the fact that their client will not return to leave a tip.

Putting The Protect Your Client's Right to Buy from You Today Principle to Work

The following questions are designed to gain a working understanding and real application in your business and in your life. Always try to answer the following questions before moving on to the next principle. This will provide you the opportunity to reflect on the value of each principle as a standalone concept. The more quality effort you apply to your answers, the better chance you will see immediate and lasting results from the value of each principle. The questions below are the same at the end of each chapter. Being cognizant of this will allow you to develop an action plan for putting the principles to work as you continue to read.

Define the key points of this principle that you will apply in your business.

Give an example of how the author demonstrated the principle.

Write three real examples of what you would say to your clients to show how you can apply this principle in your business.

Define three plans to exemplify ways that this principle will increase the quality of your selling process, margins, volume, and relationship with your clients.

Write an analogy of how this principle would apply outside of business.

NINETEEN

BE NICE

Be Nice!

Be nice to your clients and your colleagues. Be nice everywhere.

You are Michael Jordan, Pele, Muhammad Ali, or any other highly recognized individual when you are in sales. You are in front of many clients who will remember you. It may be that you speak to so many clients that you can't remember them all, but they only have to remember you. You are observed outside of the work place and still you are being judged by your behavior. If a future client sees you getting upset at the grocery store, a sporting event, or even at a PTA meeting, you are still being judged.

A client once asked about wearing business logo-wear (like an embroidered polo shirt) to work. As a consultant for sales we advised him of our primary objective when dressing for work: Dress the way your client would perceive a professional they would want to buy from would look. This could mean suit, shirt and tie, or business casual. We always advise clients to dress in the appropriate clothes for the job. The client said, "All that is fine, but I don't want my salespeople to wear company logo-wear." When asked why, he replied, "I don't want my people going to the bars and behaving inappropriately while representing our company."

This is a huge conflict of interest. Here we, as a sales training company, advise our clients to put on their name badge before they leave the house and don't take it off until they get home. We hope they are seen at the coffee shop on their way to work and at the grocery store on the way home. We want them to be a walking billboard for their business. We know that they are very approachable outside the workplace where the clients don't feel as threatened when asking questions about the product. From a marketing point of view, a name badge and company logo-wear are the same.

A side note for business owners and managers: The larger question that this business owner had to address was, why did he continue to employ people he is not happy with or is afraid would misrepresent his business? As a business owner, if you have concerns about how an individual will represent you in public, don't hire this person! As a business owner, if a salesperson doesn't represent you correctly, first write them up and clearly identify and isolate the problem. Next, outline a strategy to fix the behavior or problem. And finally, if your employee does not comply to the correct standards of the business, let them go.

This principle is a life choice. If you chose to be nice to others, it will come back to you the same way. If you are normally an intense focused individual, your challenge will be to lighten up before working with others. If you are working on a deadline and snap at the next person who just wants to ask you a question, you will be perceived as not being nice. Remember that your next client doesn't know what is going on in your life and shouldn't pay the price for your bad day.

If you don't choose to make being nice a life choice for yourself, do it for your clients. In the movie *Road House,* the character Dalton delivers an essential message to his bouncers on how he wants his clients treated. While this is aimed toward the clients who are getting out of line, nevertheless, it applies in the sales industry. Dalton explains that he has three rules. First, expect the unexpected and be ready for anything. Second, take it outside. Never allow an unhappy client to disturb all of the others from having a good time. And third, BE NICE![5] No matter what they say, smile and be nice.

Remember, you are in the public eye. You are watched everywhere you go and you are representing your business and industry. So be nice to your clients, your colleagues, your managers, your business owner and everyone else. Remember it is hard not to like people who are always nice!

5   *Road House*. Dir. Rowdy Herrington. Perf. Patrick Swayze, Kelly Lynch, and Sam Elliott. United Artists, 1989. Film.

Putting The Be Nice Principle to Work

The following questions are designed to gain a working understanding and real application in your business and in your life. Always try to answer the following questions before moving on to the next principle. This will provide you the opportunity to reflect on the value of each principle as a standalone concept. The more quality effort you apply to your answers, the better chance you will see immediate and lasting results from the value of each principle. The questions below are the same at the end of each chapter. Being cognizant of this will allow you to develop an action plan for putting the principles to work as you continue to read.

Define the key points of this principle that you will apply in your business.

Give an example of how the author demonstrated the principle.

Write three real examples of what you would say to your clients to show how you can apply this principle in your business.

Define three plans to exemplify ways that this principle will increase the quality of your selling process, margins, volume, and relationship with your clients.

Write an analogy of how this principle would apply outside of business.

TWENTY

HAVE FUN

This principle is critical for the longevity of your career. It's been said that the greater the sophistication of your work, the greater the need for simplicity of play. In your fast-paced, pressure-filled days, are you taking the time to have fun? Many work cultures take breaks to toss quarters, shoot baskets, throw footballs, or even just go for a walk to the coffee shop. What is your release?

When everyone has been focusing for days on the job, it would not be uncommon at Sobel University for an employee to break into song, and then ask their coworkers when it came out and to name the group singing. For example try this lyric, "Sing, sing a song. Make it simple to last your whole life long. Don't worry that it's not good enough for anyone else to hear. Just sing, sing a song."[6] With that song in your head, think of the paradigm shift to fun at your workplace. If you can't sing well, it even makes it more fun to sing out loud and laugh at yourself while continuing to sing. Now you are having fun!

6   Raposo, Joe. *Sing.* The Carpenters. Richard and Karen Carpenter, 1973. Vinyl recording.

The great philosopher Mary Poppins has been known to say, "In every job that must be done there is an element of fun. You find the fun and snap! The job's a game."[7] When you can have fun with clients and all of your coworkers, you may not even realize that you are at work.

It was Confucius who said, "Choose a job you love, and you will never have to work a day in your life."[8] When you look forward to going to work it's like you are young again and going to school for the first time. You can't wait to see what the new day brings.

This having fun principle is frequently substantiated at Sobel University live courses. Often, a heckler will ask a question that serves as a filibuster to lengthen the course to a point of ineffectiveness. It is not uncommon to watch the trainer start to answer and then go a different direction completely. Maybe even quote a well-known movie in the answer to get the group back to having fun and back on course. When you know and believe in this principle, no one can take you off your game.

A retired PGA player once asked a struggling golfer why he played golf. The golfer quickly replied, "I play golf to relax and have fun." The golf pro said in rebuttal, "No, you have to relax to play good golf and then you will have more fun." That advice changed the golfer's game completely. Now the golfer was singing while walking up the fairway, and released all

7   *Mary Poppins*. Dir. Robert Stevenson. Perf. Julie Andrews, Dick Van Dyke, David Tomlinson, and Glynis Johns. Buena Vista Distribution Co., 1964. Film.
8   Confucius, and D.C Lau. *The Analects*. London: Penguin, 2003. Print.

their work pressure before coming to play. Their game and life had noticeable improvements because of this release activity.

This principle brings out the eternal optimist that already exists in each of us. It takes us to our happy place where creativity can flourish. When you are having fun you are uninhibited by guidelines and the status quo. As you continue to have fun you will find that it is impossible to have fun without smiling, and smiles are contagious.

Putting The Have Fun
Principle to Work

The following questions are designed to gain a working understanding and real application in your business and in your life. Always try to answer the following questions before moving on to the next principle. This will provide you the opportunity to reflect on the value of each principle as a standalone concept. The more quality effort you apply to your answers, the better chance you will see immediate and lasting results from the value of each principle. The questions below are the same at the end of each chapter. Being cognizant of this will allow you to develop an action plan for putting the principles to work as you continue to read.

Define the key points of this principle that you will apply in your business.

Give an example of how the author demonstrated the principle.

Write three real examples of what you would say to your clients to show how you can apply this principle in your business.

Define three plans to exemplify ways that this principle will increase the quality of your selling process, margins, volume, and relationship with your clients.

Write an analogy of how this principle would apply outside of business.

TWENTY-ONE

YOU HAVE A CHOICE

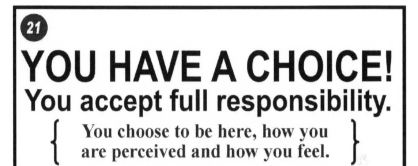

Many young people, and young at heart, push the envelope because of their no-fear and bulletproof attitudes. While this aggressive lust for life has served them in social opportunities, advancement at work and being recognized as a leader who gets things done, there is a measurable cost.

While in a defensive driving course, the instructor delivered a life-changing message that was able to identify this cost. Picture enrollment at this driving course. Everyone there was sent by a judge for speeding. The judge was hoping to help make paradigm shifts that would save lives. The enrollees were there to get a speeding ticket waived or reduced. The class was made up of all professional drivers who needed to continue driving to keep their jobs. Truck drivers, taxi drivers, bus drivers and of course people in outside sales composed the class.

The instructor walked in and explained that he would sign each release form at five o'clock on the dot, and it was only nine in the morning now. He explained that you just had to be there all day and watch movies depicting gruesome accidents that were caused by excessive speed on the roadways. He said that if you feel asleep, he didn't care, you just had to put in your time.

Then before turning on the first movie, he turned to the chalkboard and wrote: YOU HAVE A CHOICE, AND YOU ACCEPT FULL RESPONSIBILITY FOR YOUR ACTIONS! He followed by saying, "If the speed limit is 55 and you choose to go 56, you are breaking the law. When you choose to break the law, you choose to accept all consequences that go with your action. It was your choice."

Wow! What a concept. Does this mean that you don't have to speed? You could actually leave earlier and drive safely with no stress of being late to an appointment? And what about the others that are affected by your actions? The other drivers you are putting in harm's way and the clients who are always early while you barely show up on time?

This principle is easily identified and exemplified in three areas in a sales department. First, YOU HAVE A CHOICE TO BE HERE. Have you ever sat and listened to someone complain about their job in the workplace? They hate their boss, their coworkers, their inventory, the marketing strategy and even their office or desk location. There is always something to complain about and somewhere else they would rather be.

If you are one of those people who hates their job that much, leave. It is your choice to be there, you could just leave. No one would blame you for leaving if you are not happy. In fact, your coworkers may just throw you a going away party to celebrate their liberation from your negative attitude that they have had to put up with for years.

If you don't want to be at work, it may be because of Principle One. Remember, in The Graph Principle, if you have appointments coming in to see you, you will have a reason to be there. So you have a choice to follow-up with your clients and build a client base. With this client base it will be difficult to not love your job. You can make a choice to want to be there by creating a reason to be.

Second, YOU HAVE A CHOICE ABOUT HOW YOU ARE PERCEIVED. A good way to examine how this concept is exemplified would be to watch how people go through the scanners at the airport TSA. No one looks forward to having to wait in line to have their body scanned. Most people are more concerned about their upcoming flight, destination, layovers, connections and business or vacation when they land. In general, TSA is considered an inconvenience and waste of time to those who know they pose no security risk. And then there are the frequent travelers. These expert travelers are easily annoyed by inexperienced travelers who make the lines move unnecessarily slow. And finally, the TSA agents who have no regard for your valuable carry-on property when they push it, slam it, throw it, drop it, open it, touch everything in it, rescan it, and eventually repack it incorrectly. Just watch the faces of the travelers whose privacy is invaded, and this doesn't even include the random pat-downs.

How are you perceived by the TSA agent while they are, by their account, just doing their job? Describing the looks on travelers' faces could fill this book. Next time you travel, try smiling and saying a kind word to every TSA agent. Will you be treated differently? Not wanting to believe that they would treat you differently because they just had a job to do is unrealistic. Being human, how the TSA people will treat you is based on many variables, most of which are out of your control. You will be treated based on how polite or impolite the last traveler was to the agent, what is going on in the agent's personal life, and how their boss is treating them that day. You will be treated differently if you smile, if you look like someone they had a bad experience with once, or if you get the professional agent who just goes by the book.

Another instructive example is watching one traveler who was focused on his valuables. His face had no expression while his eyes never left his bags on the belt. He focused on each item as he carefully repacked what was opened and carefully lifted his property to leave. It was at that moment, one TSA agent said, "I hope you have a better day." To this the traveler replied, "What do you mean? I'm having a great day today. There was no traffic on my drive in, I was just upgraded to first class on my flight, the TSA line was short, and I get to see my favorite client in a few hours. So far, I'm having a great day!" His focus on his belongings was misinterpreted by the TSA agent.

How you are perceived is greatly influenced by you. How you dress, your level of grooming, your facial expressions, your grammar and word choice, your body language, your mood, how you treat others in public, your tone of voice, your level of interest, your speed of movement and your reaction to conditions all make up what others see and how they react to you. Ask yourself, do I care about how I am perceived? If you truly don't care, you shouldn't care about what consequences you will face for the message you just delivered.

And third, YOU HAVE A CHOICE ABOUT HOW YOU FEEL. As we get older, something always hurts. The funny thing about this is that we only feel what hurts the most. We may have many aches and pains but how we deal with them will affect our ability to perform in the workplace. You will never find a top salesperson distracted with pain when in a sales presentation. The focus on what they need to deliver will become their top-of-mind concern until the presentation is complete. Then the pain will return.

With knee surgery two days away and pain at a level 9, hardly able to breathe, the recording studio had no feelings when it expected the injured artist to perform. The studio was booked six months out, and there were deadlines to meet. The artist focused on the quality of his presentation and the expense of retakes with no time available in the foreseeable future. The show must go on! Twelve hours later, when the recording was complete with A+ work, the artist relaxed and the pain returned. His knee was so swollen he had to get help cutting his pants off when he returned home.

We have a unique way of blocking out pain when focused on something else. Top salespeople and athletes get this. Average and below average salespeople don't get this. They let themselves be distracted to the point of not wanting to talk to clients. If you are paid on commission, you are taking yourself out of commission. Within reason, you have a choice about how you feel. There are some pains that have to be dealt with urgently and now. These are not the ones we are referring to in this chapter.

If you have many friends in their 80's and 90's, it is easy to see how you will want to age. They all have pain. Some are grumpy and let you know that life is horrible and only want to talk about what hurts. Others, while in the same type of pain, are happy to see you and genuinely want to know how you are doing. They always have a smile on their face and are happy to be included and valued. They know the mile you are walking, they have been there and miss the action. They always have kind words for you and care when there is no motive or payback possibility. They have chosen how they feel!

As a salesperson, you have probably been on your way to the washroom and stopped by a client who has a question about your product. Three hours later, after the sale is made, you remind yourself you were on your way to the washroom. You were just about to sit and have lunch and fight off that hunger headache and you notice a client not being helped. Three hours later, you eat that cold lunch and start to fight off that headache that you forgot you had. These are everyday stories for top salespeople.

128

It is more than alright to admit you are in the wrong profession and make a change. Salespeople have to be available when their clients are ready for service. When your client comes to your business, they don't care that this is your lunchtime, they just want service now. Working once with an employee who had to eat at a certain time and in a certain place, it became apparent that he would never be in sales. He could work a service schedule, but never with retail clients. To be not just effective in sales, but to be great, you have to choose to put your clients first.

Putting The You Have a Choice Principle to Work

The following questions are designed to gain a working understanding and real application in your business and in your life. Always try to answer the following questions before moving on to the next principle. This will provide you the opportunity to reflect on the value of each principle as a standalone concept. The more quality effort you apply to your answers, the better chance you will see immediate and lasting results from the value of each principle. The questions below are the same at the end of each chapter. Being cognizant of this will allow you to develop an action plan for putting the principles to work as you continue to read.

Define the key points of this principle that you will apply in your business.

Give an example of how the author demonstrated the principle.

Write three real examples of what you would say to your clients to show how you can apply this principle in your business.

Define three plans to exemplify ways that this principle will increase the quality of your selling process, margins, volume, and relationship with your clients.

Write an analogy of how this principle would apply outside of business.

TWENTY-TWO

NO ONE LEAVES UNHAPPY

If a client leaves your business unhappy, they will tell ten friends who will tell ten more friends, and in a month more than one hundred people will be unhappy with your business. This was the message that was pounded into our heads at every morning sales meeting. At that time our managers were right in what they said, but as time went by their message became outdated. As more and more people communicate with instant messages, Facebook, Twitter and smartphones, if a client leaves unhappy today, three thousand of their friends may know of their problems with you in less than five minutes.

Today, your client may say bad things about you and their sister who has never met you may write a negative review. Modern media and social communication have given a voice to people who are sometimes not qualified to be speaking. However, we still have to deal and live with the outcomes. While we know what is right, what is right is sometimes different in the minds of our consumers.

A good rule to follow would be to put a price or value on what it cost to bring the client into your business. For example, take the amount of money that you make and divide it by the number of clients who make a purchase. If you find that you pay $500 per unit sold in advertising, you may not want that client to leave and infect your right to bring others into your business. To fix a negative reputation could double your cost in advertising.

If you think of your client as a $500 opportunity made or lost, you must take the appropriate actions before this client can leave unhappy. As a rule, if you think your client is unhappy and you have tried to do everything you can to fix how they feel without positive results, get help. Find another salesperson or manager who can identify and isolate the problem for immediate remediation. In this example it is a $1,000 swing in money made or lost plus the immeasurable cost of those who the unhappy clients infect.

Putting The No One Leaves Unhappy Principle to Work

The following questions are designed to gain a working understanding and real application in your business and in your life. Always try to answer the following questions before moving on to the next principle. This will provide you the opportunity to reflect on the value of each principle as a standalone concept. The more quality effort you apply to your answers, the better chance you will see immediate and lasting results from the value of each principle. The questions below are the same at the end of each chapter. Being cognizant of this will allow you to develop an action plan for putting the principles to work as you continue to read.

Define the key points of this principle that you will apply in your business.

Give an example of how the author demonstrated the principle.

Write three real examples of what you would say to your clients to show how you can apply this principle in your business.

Define three plans to exemplify ways that this principle will increase the quality of your selling process, margins, volume, and relationship with your clients.

Write an analogy of how this principle would apply outside of business.

TWENTY-THREE

THOU SHALL NOT DEFAME ONE'S CLIENTS

② THOU SHALL NOT DEFAME ONES CLIENT!

If you don't help your client, your competition will.

A language that should have never been invented is Automobilese. This language includes such choice words like: mooch, bust-out, roach, get-me-done, humpty, in the ditch, one-legger, moon booter, and upside down. Unfortunately, every one of these words defines clients in a negative tone. As explained in other principles, without our clients we would not exist. So it begs the question: Why would you make up words that negatively depict the people who keep you employed? And what of the other clients who hear you speak in this way?

To try to explain why words are made up will be logical, but negative depictions of our clients is inexcusable. At some point, words like ruminant were invented to shorten a description or turn many words into one word that describes a group. Ruminant is quicker than saying cloven-hoofed cud-chewing quadrupeds like cattle, bison, deer and the like. It is not a derogatory term, just a descriptive word.

In business we use words like opportunity cost in the same way. Opportunity cost is quicker to say than: the money or other benefits lost when pursuing a particular course of action instead of a mutually exclusive alternative. We should use words to shorten and increase the quality of communication when it benefits your clients. Conversely, the use of big words to make ourselves look impressive or put down others is just as insulting as calling your clients names like stupid. This would still be defaming your clients.

A simple way to sum up this principle would be to not just value your client, but to appreciate them as well. If you enjoy the time you spend with your clients you will not be working, rather, you will just be spending time with a friend. If you continue to defame and put down your client, remember the following: "If you don't help your client, someone else will."

Putting The Thou Shall Not Defame One's Clients Principle to Work

The following questions are designed to gain a working understanding and real application in your business and in your life. Always try to answer the following questions before moving on to the next principle. This will provide you the opportunity to reflect on the value of each principle as a standalone concept. The more quality effort you apply to your answers, the better chance you will see immediate and lasting results from the value of each principle. The questions below are the same at the end of each chapter. Being cognizant of this will allow you to develop an action plan for putting the principles to work as you continue to read.

Define the key points of this principle that you will apply in your business.

Give an example of how the author demonstrated the principle.

Write three real examples of what you would say to your clients to show how you can apply this principle in your business.

Define three plans to exemplify ways that this principle will increase the quality of your selling process, margins, volume, and relationship with your clients.

Write an analogy of how this principle would apply outside of business.

TWENTY-FOUR

BE MEMORABLE

Will your clients not just think of you, but think of you *first*, and then only think of *you*.

What makes you memorable? Be Memorable means both that you are easy to remember and that you are worth remembering. If you are easy to remember, but do not do anything special or worth being remembered for, you will be forgotten. What will be remembered will be what is important to your client, and not what you think was important. Many salespeople grow what they perceive as stylish facial hair or get tattoos and piercings. If your client doesn't share your views about style, they may actually try to forget you quickly.

To be memorable in sales is easier than you may think. The quickest way is to give the best presentation your client has ever seen in their life. Odds are that your client has never been given a good presentation. This is explained well in Chapter Eighteen; when you are the best your client has ever seen, you will not only be remembered, but they will be excited to send you referrals.

Another way to Be Memorable is to always wear clothes that make your clients smile. There was a salesperson who always wore a different Disney tie. He was able to build a client base of people who remembered him not always by name, but the guy with the Disney ties. While the ties made people remember him, his actions made him memorable. He was always G-Rated, and looked for ways to perform random acts of kindness.

When you think back to a teacher, coach or advisor, why do you remember some and not others? It could be how they were role models, taught you a valuable lesson or simply said something that you will never forget. These memorable mentors seemed to all have shown up at a time when you needed them. How could it be that they all magically appeared? Could it be that you were looking for answers and found them? Or were you just lucky? It could be a little of both.

When your client comes to you they are looking for answers. Will you be their mentor, their teacher, and coach who will give them the service that they do not know how to ask for? Will you care about your client and help them achieve their goals with your product? If you take the time to really be significant to your client, you will Be Memorable.

The salespeople who are most memorable are consistent and transparent in their message. To be a certain way in front of one client and a different way in front of others would be like the salesperson is lying to themselves. If you are a good service provider and believe in what you bring to your clients, you will only want to deliver the same top quality to all of your clients all of the time. When you care about the well-being of your clients, your clients will know.

GIVE YOURSELF THE FOLLOWING QUIZ:

Will my clients think of me when I am not there?

Will my clients think of me first?

Will my clients only think of me in regard to my product?

Do my clients think I care about them as more than a sale?

Will my clients trust me with their
friends and family (referrals)?

Will my clients speak well of me to others?

Do my clients ask how I am doing, and wait for an answer?

What have I done for my client that they
have not experienced before?

What is it exactly that my client will remember me for?

Does my client want me to be successful?

Does my client go out of their way to only buy from me?

Does my client enjoy the time they spend with me?

IF THE ABOVE ARE EASILY ANSWERED "YES," THEN YOU ARE MEMORABLE!

Putting The Be Memorable Principle to Work

The following questions are designed to gain a working understanding and real application in your business and in your life. Always try to answer the following questions before moving on to the next principle. This will provide you the opportunity to reflect on the value of each principle as a standalone concept. The more quality effort you apply to your answers, the better chance you will see immediate and lasting results from the value of each principle. The questions below are the same at the end of each chapter. Being cognizant of this will allow you to develop an action plan for putting the principles to work as you continue to read.

Define the key points of this principle that you will apply in your business.

Give an example of how the author demonstrated the principle.

Write three real examples of what you would say to your clients to show how you can apply this principle in your business.

Define three plans to exemplify ways that this principle will increase the quality of your selling process, margins, volume, and relationship with your clients.

Write an analogy of how this principle would apply outside of business.

140

TWENTY-FIVE

ALLOW YOUR CLIENTS TO GIVE YOU A GOOD TIP

25 Allow your clients to give you a good tip.

Clients want good service and are willing to pay for it.

At a restaurant, a family sat down and ordered iced tea. The waiter noticed that only the pink packets of sweetener were used. When he came back to take the order he refilled the teas and replaced the sugar bowl with just the pink packets. Later when he checked on how the food was prepared he asked how the sauce was that he had recommended on the halibut. When the client said it was outstanding, he delivered an extra bowl of sauce without the client having to ask. The drinks were never empty and desert samples were brought over to taste before ordering. Needless to say, the waiter received an outstanding tip!

Ask yourself, have you ever gone out to a restaurant and hoped for bad service so you could save money on a tip? Most people go out for the service. They don't want to cook and clean. They may be celebrating a special event. They want good service and are willing to pay for it. This principle is about allowing your clients to give you a good tip.

When should you not expect to get a good tip? First, when your client gives you a budget and you proceed to sell something to them that is above their budget. If their budget is $50,000 and you make them love a product that is $55,000, any money they had to give you for a tip (commission) is not available. In fact, if you push your client out of their budget you will either lose the sale, or if they purchase, they may hate you for pushing them into too much product. In this case you will not get a good tip because the client has no money left after buying the product to pay your commission.

Another time not to expect a good tip is when the client orders beef and you serve fish. If you don't listen to your client you will never be able to serve them correctly. Sometimes, listening has everything to do with taking the time to ask questions. If you are a food server, do you ask if there are any allergies that should be brought to the attention of the chief? If you ask, and the client says they have a food allergy, and you don't check the food, if it is prepared wrong don't expect a tip!

It is the same thing if you don't take the time to understand your client's wants, needs and budget in the product selection step in your selling process. If you skip this step, you may find yourself showing products that your clients will have no interest in purchasing.

Many salespeople have heard many clients ask, "Now you are going to make some money on this sale aren't you?" That is the client's way of asking if you will be compensated for your good work. Remember that your clients have come to you for service and are willing to pay for it. It is too easy in this day and age for your clients to purchase online. They have gone out of their way to come to you. Don't let them down by not giving them better service than they expect.

Putting The Allow Your Clients to Give You a Good Tip Principle to Work

The following questions are designed to gain a working understanding and real application in your business and in your life. Always try to answer the following questions before moving on to the next principle. This will provide you the opportunity to reflect on the value of each principle as a standalone concept. The more quality effort you apply to your answers, the better chance you will see immediate and lasting results from the value of each principle. The questions below are the same at the end of each chapter. Being cognizant of this will allow you to develop an action plan for putting the principles to work as you continue to read.

Define the key points of this principle that you will apply in your business.

Give an example of how the author demonstrated the principle.

Write three real examples of what you would say to your clients to show how you can apply this principle in your business.

Define three plans to exemplify ways that this principle will increase the quality of your selling process, margins, volume, and relationship with your clients.

Write an analogy of how this principle would apply outside of business.

TWENTY-SIX

BE PREDICTABLE

Be Predictable
To everyone everywhere

In drivers education we were taught to engage our turn signal two full telephone poles prior to turning. This was so that the drivers behind us would know what to expect. Later we found that most other drivers (hopefully not you) signaled late, or sometimes not at all. When we are predictable, others around us can see what we are doing, and what we plan to do next. This allows others to compensate for our shortcomings, possibly help us, and be stress free with no surprises.

When you have a selling system, you have a predictable process where others know where you are at all times. There are three people in your business who will impact your selling system. First are sales managers. If your managers know where you are in your presentation, they can help you advance the sale. They will also know when you hit a stumbling block. For example, if you go to show a product that fits your client's wants, needs, and budget and your manager sees that you are jumping from one product to the next, the manager knows that you need help.

Second, your clients need to see that you are predictable. It is very likely that all of your clients' experience with salespeople so far in their lives has been built on a certain lack of trust. Let's face it, if the client had a trusting relationship with another salesperson who sells a similar product, the client would be buying there. When your clients know and agree with what you are going to do for them next, they instantly become more comfortable with what is now their purchasing process. Much of the stress in your relationship with your clients comes from you being unpredictable, which in turn forces the client become guarded. When you are predictable, your clients will begin to trust you and the service you provide.

The third group of people is other salespeople and coworkers. When you are not predictable and you need to turn one of your clients to another salesperson, the salesperson who takes the turn will not be effective. For another to effectively help your client they need to know what you have already said and done. For example, if you skip the step where you sit down and figure out a client's budget and race straight out to a product it will be likely that the product you are showing will not fit the client's budget. If you end up turning this client to another salesperson they will assume that you didn't skip the budget step and not know why the client will not close. If this continues, no other salesperson will ever want to help you! For all of the same reasons other coworkers need to know that you have done your part of the selling process as well.

When you are predictable the increased communication in your business will provide outstanding service for your clients. You will enjoy a more stress-free selling experience with all who are involved with the process. Your repeat and referral business will flourish because your clients will trust you and trust that you will treat their friends in the same professional manner.

Putting The Be Predictable Principle to Work

The following questions are designed to gain a working understanding and real application in your business and in your life. Always try to answer the following questions before moving on to the next principle. This will provide you the opportunity to reflect on the value of each principle as a standalone concept. The more quality effort you apply to your answers, the better chance you will see immediate and lasting results from the value of each principle. The questions below are the same at the end of each chapter. Being cognizant of this will allow you to develop an action plan for putting the principles to work as you continue to read.

Define the key points of this principle that you will apply in your business.

Give an example of how the author demonstrated the principle.

Write three real examples of what you would say to your clients to show how you can apply this principle in your business.

Define three plans to exemplify ways that this principle will increase the quality of your selling process, margins, volume, and relationship with your clients.

Write an analogy of how this principle would apply outside of business.

TWENTY-SEVEN

KOBAYASHI MARU

Kobayashi Maru
The no-win scenario does not exist.

For those readers who follow the *Star Trek* series, the Kobayashi Maru should sound familiar. If you don't, it is the test administered to captain candidates to see how they handle the stress of being faced with a no-win scenario. As it is believed that the no-win scenario is a very real and frequent occurrence in all leadership positions, one is expected to prepare, if not train, on how to handle defeat.[9] The premise that losing is an option will not serve a salesperson well. If in fact you believe too soon in your sales process that your client will not purchase, it will become a self-fulfilling prophecy.

Sobel University training teaches that the second you believe that your client will not purchase, you are right! Your presentation will develop short cuts and the quality and effort will be compromised. This will lead to a no sale. Have you ever heard a client say at the end of a presentation that they had no intentions of making a purchase today? They made the purchase because the salesperson did not believe

9   *Star Trek: The Wrath of Khan*. Dir. Nicholas Meyer. Perf. William Shatner and Leonard Nimoy. Paramount, 1982. Film.

in the no-win scenario and gave the client the presentation that the client needed to feel comfortable and knowledgeable enough to make the purchasing decision.

A frequently used business term that can influence this principle is opportunity cost. This would imply that when you select one course over the other, there is a cost in the path that was not selected. In the no-win scenario just because you select one path doesn't mean the other path is shut down. It just means you select the best way of winning now and leave the other opportunity for another time when it may be a more advantageous selection.

The challenge is not to lock on so tightly to one option that you limit your ability to see the alternatives. Frequently our opinions get in the way of seeing clearly. In Sobel University courses, when students focus on their current way of selling they can't always see or comprehend the new material that is being introduced. When this occurs, the instructor tells everyone to memorize everything they see in the room that is brown. The instructor has the class close their eyes and repeat in their heads all that they saw that is brown. Then the class is told to say out loud everything that they saw that is blue. The room becomes so quiet that you could hear a pin drop. The epiphany in this exercise is when the students open their eyes and see the name card right in front of them is blue.

**When we lock on to the way we see the world,
we often lock out all other possibilities.**

This will not serve you well in looking for the best alternative.

Another secret to executing this principle is to not get trapped into a long deliberation over a simple decision or one that requires immediate attention with a deadline. While there are always options in what appears to be a no-win scenario, making no decision is a decision. Many salespeople find themselves ineffective as opportunities pass them by while they are thinking. Too many times ineffective salespeople and leaders fall into the trap of analysis to paralysis.

When training sales managers and leaders in a sales department it is critical to empower them to make a decision. What helps is to ask them to think of three alternatives that could work, and execute one! The mistake would be to always wait for their supervisor to help them make a decision. No decision as a decision could lead to poor service, a lost sale, or just nothing happening at all. With this concept of selecting three options or alternatives, a review will prove to enhance productivity. When you review the situation with a manager, you will see your three choices, and your manager may show you three that you didn't consider. This way when you are in the same situation in the future, you will have more ways to make the best decision.

Having alternatives means that you have already taken the time to recognize them. It may look like top salespeople make things up as they go, but the preparation, training, and the synthesis of alternative plans was all done before they entered the sales arena. What looks creative may be a well thought out and rehearsed presentation. Depending on the product you sell, there may be an unlimited number of ways to put a deal together.

In all of the job descriptions ever written for salespeople, nowhere will you read, "Just give up, there is no way to make a living on commission in this job." To execute the no-win scenario, you must start by believing you can win. If your path is blocked, find another way. Giving up is not an option. Stay focused and calm. Open your mind to see all of your options. And finally, make a decision and execute your plan.

Putting The Kobayashi Maru Principle to Work

The following questions are designed to gain a working understanding and real application in your business and in your life. Always try to answer the following questions before moving on to the next principle. This will provide you the opportunity to reflect on the value of each principle as a standalone concept. The more quality effort you apply to your answers, the better chance you will see immediate and lasting results from the value of each principle. The questions below are the same at the end of each chapter. Being cognizant of this will allow you to develop an action plan for putting the principles to work as you continue to read.

Define the key points of this principle that you will apply in your business.

Give an example of how the author demonstrated the principle.

Write three real examples of what you would say to your clients to show how you can apply this principle in your business.

Define three plans to exemplify ways that this principle will increase the quality of your selling process, margins, volume, and relationship with your clients.

Write an analogy of how this principle would apply outside of business.

153

TWENTY-EIGHT

START WITH AN HEAD

 Start with an empty head

Don't let your action plan get in your way of listening.

When you begin your sales presentation, you must acknowledge that your client came to you with the idea that they want or need your product. Many salespeople get in the way of the client achieving their goals. To be able to get on the right track, your client's track, you must empty your head and listen to why your client is here; their wants, their needs, and their budget. If you want to help them purchase, you can't have any preconceived plans or you may find yourself locked onto the color brown as explained in the previous chapter. As professionals we can't let our action plans get in the way of truly listening.

As we listen to our clients with an empty head, what message being delivered to us is the most important? Let's say that you ask your client a question and they respond in three sentences. The first sentence is their immediate reaction to what you said. The second sentence could be described as the client thinking out loud. And the third sentence is their final thought on your original statement. Which of the three responses will be the most important to you? Is it option one, their immediate reaction, option two, their thinking out loud, or option three, their final thought? In class, we hear students select all three different answers. The correct answer is option three, their final thought.

The challenge for a vast number of salespeople is their selection of option one, the client's immediate reaction. When this occurs, the salesperson starts reacting to the client's reaction and never really hears the client's final thought. Reactions to reactions to reactions, may never get to the point. Also, it is near impossible for you the salesperson to listen to the still-speaking client when you are preoccupied planning what you are going to say next. It is good for your client to see that you are listening to their complete thought and taking the time to give a considerate and respectful response.

In effective communications your presentation should start by repeating what your client just said to you. This will allow your client to see that you care about what your client feels is important to share. It will help you clarify what your client said so you can be sure to go the right direction with your presentation. Repeating their ideas will also allow you to buy time to consider the best alternatives for your client. This buying time works because it takes a very small percentage of your brain's capacity to repeat what your client is saying. The rest of your brain is working to develop a plan. Start

With an Empty Head means that you are willing to truly listen before you engage a sales plan. By actively listening you will gain respect as you select the best path to help your client purchase.

A karate master with five black belts from five different disciplines went to Bruce Lee and asked him to teach him his karate. Bruce Lee said that he could not teach his discipline to the master. When the master said he could learn anything and Bruce Lee still refused, the master was educated on why he could not be taught. Bruce Lee took a glass of water and one of tea. He explained that the water was his karate and the tea was what the master has learned. The tea was a blend of five different disciplines. He explained that if he poured all the water into the tea, the water would not be the same. Both the water and the tea are pure and good by themselves; however, if you mix them together you have neither the good water nor the good tea.

To learn one thing well, you must learn it as a stand-alone concept.

It is impossible to learn with an empty head if you are blending or combining concepts. It is more likely that both concepts will become compromised and prove to be ineffective. To learn one new concept, all other thoughts on the area of consideration must be set aside or erased. This is where the concept of you can't teach an old dog new tricks comes into play. While you are trying to give the dog new information, the dog is confusing it with the old trick and unable to learn. This plays out into your muscle memory when you greet a new client. If you think you know what the client wants because they remind you of another client and you skip your product selection step, you will not be starting with an empty head. You will find quickly that your action plan is getting in the way of listening to what this new and unique client needs.

One of the most common plots in the movie industry deals with the transformation and evolution of the human spirit. To become a Jedi in *Star Wars*, one of the people in *Avatar*, or just the *Karate Kid* you must empty your head to really listen so learning can occur. In the movies, as in real life, this takes courage. You are asked to stay calm and not lock onto or react to any concept or stimulus until all of the information is presented and processed. As in the movies, with practice you will learn to empty your head and eventually find great peace in helping your clients achieve their goals with your products.

Putting The Start With an Empty Head Principle to Work

The following questions are designed to gain a working understanding and real application in your business and in your life. Always try to answer the following questions before moving on to the next principle. This will provide you the opportunity to reflect on the value of each principle as a standalone concept. The more quality effort you apply to your answers, the better chance you will see immediate and lasting results from the value of each principle. The questions below are the same at the end of each chapter. Being cognizant of this will allow you to develop an action plan for putting the principles to work as you continue to read.

Define the key points of this principle that you will apply in your business.

Give an example of how the author demonstrated the principle.

Write three real examples of what you would say to your clients to show how you can apply this principle in your business.

Define three plans to exemplify ways that this principle will increase the quality of your selling process, margins, volume, and relationship with your clients.

Write an analogy of how this principle would apply outside of business.

TWENTY-NINE

YOU ARE THE PHYSICIAN

 You are the physician.

The client needs your professional diagnosis.

About one hundred years ago if your elbow was hurting, you would go to see your family doctor. This wasn't the dark ages, but the physicians back then had limited diagnostic tools. Then after an examination if the doctor believed that you had a torn tendon they would cut into your elbow to see for sure. Back then, the doctor only had your description of the problem to determine if surgery was required.

Now jump forward to the present. Your elbow hurts so you consult an online medical dictionary. You type in the description of the problem and you determine that you have a torn tendon. You go to see a doctor and point to the painful spot and describe the torn tendon you have in the exact terms you learned from the online medical dictionary. The doctor turns to his computer and types in your symptoms. Of course, his computer confirms what your computer said, so he schedules surgery. Once you are cut open, the doctor determines that you do not have a torn tendon.

In the last two paragraphs the outcome is the same. Luckily, modern medicine does not allow you to self-diagnose. Today, the process would be after your general practitioner suspects a problem, they would refer you to a specialist like an orthopedic surgeon. The surgeon would use tools like an MRI to see the problem area more clearly from the inside out. Before the surgery would be scheduled, you would be given alternatives, physical therapy, and the surgeon would show his findings to a colleague to confirm. You would meet with an anesthesiologist to determine the best option for putting you under and waking you up. And finally, you would outline a recovery plan.

As a sales professional, you act as the physician. When it comes to your product, the clients need your professional diagnosis. Your clients will still consult the internet and jump to all kinds of conclusions based on what they read and what other untrained people are saying. One example was exposed after speaking at a "How to Purchase" seminar for clients in the RV industry. An RV owner of three months acknowledged that he purchased online and had his new travel trailer delivered to his lake property. What he said next is what makes his case memorable. He said, "Check out my butt!" After looking at him and his wife next to him oddly, he continued by saying, "No, seriously, check out my butt. It's so big that it doesn't fit through the door of the bathroom. I bought an RV that I can't even use the toilet."

This couple self-diagnosed and purchased clearly the wrong product. They would have been better served to work with a professional who could see their challenges and present them with options that would work for their circumstances. While the internet is a great research tool, salespeople can't rely on the information their clients find to paint the whole picture. Many of the products that are viewed even on a factory website are no longer available at the retail level. As a sales professional, you must do the full diagnostic in your business, and when possible get a second opinion. In the sales industry this is called product selection and manager checkpoint.

One other obstacle that must be kept in check would be your need for speed. A young doctor was bragging about his accomplishments of treating more than twenty patients in a single day. Of course, his supervising senior doctor asked how he could diagnose so many people accurately without really listening to them. The young doctor's quick answer was that he ran tests and made decisions. The supervisor just scratched his head and said, "You are going to miss something if you don't slow down and really listen." The young doctor immediately explained that the hospital administration appreciated the efficiency and productivity of his work.

Of course a senior doctor doesn't get into that position without reason, and the young doctor ran into a problem the next day. A lady that he had treated for pain and released was now back and barely alive. Finally taking the time, the young doctor sat down next to the patient and started asking questions about her life and really listening. He found that she had purchased homemade plates and was eating off them daily. He was able to determine that the plates were made in a way that was making her ill. After slowing down and listening to our clients, we will drastically increase our ability to show the right product.

In this principle, You are the Physician: Your client needs your professional diagnosis. They don't know what questions to ask, how your product is made to fit their needs, or even enough to make a purchasing decision. You can count on the fact that your client is not confident enough to purchase with their self-diagnosis and the fast sales presentations they may have already received or they would not be in front of you!

Putting The You are the Physician Principle to Work

The following questions are designed to gain a working understanding and real application in your business and in your life. Always try to answer the following questions before moving on to the next principle. This will provide you the opportunity to reflect on the value of each principle as a standalone concept. The more quality effort you apply to your answers, the better chance you will see immediate and lasting results from the value of each principle. The questions below are the same at the end of each chapter. Being cognizant of this will allow you to develop an action plan for putting the principles to work as you continue to read.

Define the key points of this principle that you will apply in your business.

Give an example of how the author demonstrated the principle.

Write three real examples of what you would say to your clients to show how you can apply this principle in your business.

Define three plans to exemplify ways that this principle will increase the quality of your selling process, margins, volume, and relationship with your clients.

Write an analogy of how this principle would apply outside of business.

THIRTY

Talk About What You Know

 Talk about what you know, not what you believe.

Your client is paying for your professional knowledge not your opinion.

While listening to a specialist in the field of neurophysiology speak of his work on the functions of the nervous system, my focus was interrupted by the person next to me who said, "Well, let me tell you what I believe." Knowing that the person next to me had no medical training immediately disqualified any and all comments she was about to profess. This was a rare opportunity to hear from one of the top physicians in their field and yet the unknowledgable, opinionated person next to me would not stop speaking. Who are you in this story? The neurophysiologist, the student, or the person who talks about what they believe with no real knowledge on the subject?

Your clients wish to pay for your professional knowledge, not your opinion! Too often salespeople feel the need to say what they think they need to say to close the deal. This is not always what your client needs to hear to make a purchasing decision. Today's clients need a teacher, not a pitch-man. To feel confident enough to purchase, the clients need the right facts. In every case your clients need an educator who speaks about the facts, and not just personal opinions.

Most salespeople have found themselves earning the trust of their client and recognizing this when the client asks, "Which one would you buy?" This question can be a slippery slope if not answered correctly. You must fight the tendency to answer by talking about your favorite product. Instead, an easy answer would be to say, "It's not what I would buy, it's what I would buy if I were you. You have small kids, mine are grown and gone. You have different needs than mine. Let's help you get the product that fits your needs, not mine."

One manager described his salesperson in this questionable way: "He has the right to remain silent, he just doesn't have the capability to remain silent." There are too many salespeople who feel that they have to fill every uncomfortable moment of silence with words to fill the void of stillness. Another way to say stillness is peace. If your presentation is peaceful and educational your clients will find satisfaction more quickly.

The title of this principle is the best and most succinct definition. TALK ABOUT WHAT YOU KNOW, NOT WHAT YOU BELIEVE. Remember, your client is paying for your professional knowledge to get them the best product to meet their needs!

Putting The Talk About What You Know Principle to Work

The following questions are designed to gain a working understanding and real application in your business and in your life. Always try to answer the following questions before moving on to the next principle. This will provide you the opportunity to reflect on the value of each principle as a standalone concept. The more quality effort you apply to your answers, the better chance you will see immediate and lasting results from the value of each principle. The questions below are the same at the end of each chapter. Being cognizant of this will allow you to develop an action plan for putting the principles to work as you continue to read.

Define the key points of this principle that you will apply in your business.

Give an example of how the author demonstrated the principle.

Write three real examples of what you would say to your clients to show how you can apply this principle in your business.

Define three plans to exemplify ways that this principle will increase the quality of your selling process, margins, volume, and relationship with your clients.

Write an analogy of how this principle would apply outside of business.

THIRTY-ONE

LOVE THE GAME

Love of the game

Train to play the whole game.

This principle is easily exemplified by watching most any athlete at the top of their professional career. They have a serious, all-business look during the game that could be confused for anger when it really is just intense focus. They may not look like they are having much fun, but they are having the time of their life. It is what they have trained for with hours and sweat equity. Top salespeople are the same. They love what they do and the time in the gym learning is as enjoyable as the game itself.

People who love sales want the ball when the game is on the line. When a client enters your business, top salespeople are always the first to get excited and can't wait for the opportunity for another sale. It is unfortunate that many people enter a sales career because it is a job, or a job they can get. These people are easily identified. They are not happy to come to work, talk to a client, or study the product, and worse than all of that, they don't get the elation or euphoria when a sale is closed.

Salespeople who love what they do enjoy the whole ride. They study their trade for hours trying not to miss one detail that could come up in a selling situation. They role-play with anyone who will give them the time so that they know what they sound like delivering a presentation at real game speed. You will never hear a top performer complain about training. They love to learn as much as playing in the game.

Because of this love of the game, top performers train to play the whole game. In any professional trade, the higher the level, the better you can expect your competition will prepare and be trained. A clerk may ring up a product, while a salesperson who sells big-ticket products may give a sales presentation that can take hours or even days. This type of sales presentation requires that a salesperson trains to play the whole game. It is not uncommon for salespeople to work through lunch or even forget they were on their way to the washroom when a client intercepts them for a three hour sales presentation.

If you study the top performers you will see a transformation in their workout schedule as they approach selling or trade shows. First they change their sleep patterns. They will put themselves on a strict schedule to get the right amount of sleep required to generate maximum rest for the game ahead. Second, they change their eating habits. They will only eat during certain times of day and not risk eating something that will slow them down or take them out of commission. The third change you will see top performers make will be in their exercise. They know they may be on their feet putting in twelve hour days at a show and can't risk being tired when the next client may be their best sale of the entire week.

The last noticeable change will be in the equipment the professional relies on to perform at their peak. Clothing and more specifically, shoes. The new shoes will come out a few days before the show so they can be tested and broken in just enough for confidence but not enough to lose the new shoe bounce. The new clothing will be prepared and tested for comfort, durability and most of all presentation. Batteries to remotes, keyboards, mouse devices, laser pointers and back-up presentations are loaded and tested. Top salespeople will leave nothing to chance that they can prepare for in advance.

As part of loving the game, top salespeople hate bench time. They hate to sit and wait for clients to come to them. They are always moving. When they are not with a client, they are target marketing, following up a lead, following up a sale, checking inventory, studying product, asking how another deal was made or lost, asking for referrals, role-playing, or just getting ready for their next presentation. This always moving should not be confused as nervous energy. It is keeping your head in the game so you can be ready for the next client. You will see professional athletes riding a stationary bike on the sideline to stay lose so they can re-enter the game at real game speed. It is hard to get fired back up if you take yourself out of the game mentally.

In this chapter, the Love of the Game speaks of study and practice time. Time must be spent in the gym rather than primarily on the field of play. Many salespeople show up to work on time and start work at the scheduled time. In studying top performers, they have a ritual that gets them ready before the game begins. Many start one to two hours before work. They say that they want the quiet time to themselves to prepare for the day's events. They typically show up early and get their studying done before anyone else shows up. Top performers don't rely on making it up as they go, rather they are prepared for all possibilities that could unfold during the sales process. They consider the time in the practice room as part of the selling process, not just the time with the client.

Finally, if you love the game, you have no excuses. Top salespeople find a way to win through perseverance. They know this means a steady persistence in their course of action while focused on a purpose, and especially in spite of difficulties, obstacles, or discouragement. They never listen to others' excuses like: They get all the good clients, The manager likes him better, The inventory stinks, The weather is bad or We don't advertise correctly.

Top salespeople focus on what they can control and don't worry about what they can't. They simply persevere.

As top professional athletes see the twilight of their careers, they are noticeably grateful for the opportunity to play the game that they love at the highest level. While most of the information in this chapter was focused on preparing and playing the game, it must be noted that the love of the game continues after the game is over. As you get closer to your retirement, you start to realize that the game was a big part of your life. Hopefully, you lived your sales life at the highest level and can retire grateful for the opportunity to play and still loving the game.

Putting The Love the Game Principle to Work

The following questions are designed to gain a working understanding and real application in your business and in your life. Always try to answer the following questions before moving on to the next principle. This will provide you the opportunity to reflect on the value of each principle as a standalone concept. The more quality effort you apply to your answers, the better chance you will see immediate and lasting results from the value of each principle. The questions below are the same at the end of each chapter. Being cognizant of this will allow you to develop an action plan for putting the principles to work as you continue to read.

Define the key points of this principle that you will apply in your business.

Give an example of how the author demonstrated the principle.

Write three real examples of what you would say to your clients to show how you can apply this principle in your business.

Define three plans to exemplify ways that this principle will increase the quality of your selling process, margins, volume, and relationship with your clients.

Write an analogy of how this principle would apply outside of business.

THIRTY-TWO

COURAGE

32 Courage

**To Say What Is Right
To Stay On Track
To Ask For The Order**

Courage, as a principle, could be a whole book by itself. So let's start by defining Courage as the quality of mind or spirit that enables a person to face difficulty without fear, and persevere with bravery. This mind or spirit starts by asking yourself, "Am I in the right line of work?" There are too many people who take a sales job who have no desire to be in sales. In order to talk to clients with a mission to sell your product, you must have the "I want to" belief in yourself to get off to the right start. As Courage is a large topic, for this chapter we will break it down into three headings: Courage to stay on track, Courage to say the right thing even if it's not comfortable, and Courage to ask for the order.

Courage to stay on track simply means that you must stick with your selling process. If your process starts with meet and greet, you must take the time to really find a safe place to communicate with your client so that they will feel comfortable giving you the right information that will aid you in helping your client purchase the product. This safe place to communicate is critical when you start asking about personal use and budget. Too often salespeople skip this step and start their greeting with: "Can I help you?" Or with: "Hi, welcome to ____ my name is ___and yours is?" These common greetings move you to the product too quickly and without enough information to provide good service. These greetings also violate the personal space of your client because you are within three feet of them before they have a chance to feel comfortable. This Courage to stay on track is actually very easy if you believe in your selling process.

Courage to say the right thing even if it's not comfortable is actually very easy if you believe in your selling process. There should be no discomfort in saying what is right. For example, if your client says they want to just look at the products without you, and your process is to show the client the product so they can get the best presentation, you don't need Courage to say the right thing. Simply explain why your process is for the client. You can use the principles of Time Frame or The Circle and Square to explain why your client may want to manage you. This will allow you to show them the right product that they want to see, with the best educational presentation.

This Courage to say the right thing even if it's not comfortable, after believing in your selling process, comes down simply to doing the right thing. This should not be a judgment call where there are different views of what is right. In sales, there should be no gray area. There is right and wrong and they are as clear as day and night. If you sell in the gray area you will quickly lose trust, and there will be confusion and frustration during the selling process and the delivery of your product. In addition, if your client buys the product because they really want it, but doesn't like you or your process, you can expect no referrals.

What makes doing the right thing so difficult is simply knowing the difference between right and wrong. Our clients and our opinions can easily get in the way of sticking to the facts. It is unfortunate when a salesperson is allowed to speak to a client before they are properly trained on the business's product and process. New salespeople may not do what is right because they don't know what is right. As instructors of sales courses, it is common to see students change their complete view of what it means to be a professional salesperson. Many students start by believing that the course will teach them how to lie and live in the gray area. The epiphany is so bright that it lights up the classroom when a student gets that we exist to help our clients get what they want with truth and integrity.

This is also exemplified when your clients come to your business after shopping your competition without the success of making a purchase. They must have been treated poorly by the last business who sells the same product or they would have already made a purchase. It will be critical to start in a safe place to communicate with a client who doesn't trust you because of what they have already experienced.

As the next chapter will reveal that The Client Is Not Always Right, you must educate the client. That is why they came to you, for the correct information that will empower them to make a purchasing decision. You should not allow yourself to be put in an uncomfortable position if you stick to your educational selling process.

And finally, Courage to ask for the order simply means that if you have done everything correctly in your selling process the close is easy and stress free. If you have to muster up the courage to ask for the order, you must not have sold the product correctly. There should be many places in your selling process where the client can stop you and say, "This is the one we want, can we buy it now?" If you build your trial closing techniques around a summary of the product (summary closing technique) and your client stops you to tell you they want to buy, then you will not need courage to ask for the order.

To summarize this principle would be to say that courage is not needed if you know, believe in, and follow your selling process. It should never take courage to do what is right. Never compromise on what you know is right and stay out of the gray area. If your client came to see you, they want to purchase your product. Today's clients have already researched online and committed the time to come to your business. It should not take courage to help your clients get what they want.

Putting The Courage Principle to Work

The following questions are designed to gain a working understanding and real application in your business and in your life. Always try to answer the following questions before moving on to the next principle. This will provide you the opportunity to reflect on the value of each principle as a standalone concept. The more quality effort you apply to your answers, the better chance you will see immediate and lasting results from the value of each principle. The questions below are the same at the end of each chapter. Being cognizant of this will allow you to develop an action plan for putting the principles to work as you continue to read.

Define the key points of this principle that you will apply in your business.

Give an example of how the author demonstrated the principle.

Write three real examples of what you would say to your clients to show how you can apply this principle in your business.

Define three plans to exemplify ways that this principle will increase the quality of your selling process, margins, volume, and relationship with your clients.

Write an analogy of how this principle would apply outside of business.

THIRTY-THREE

THE CLIENT IS NOT ALWAYS RIGHT

When this principle was first introduced to experienced salespeople, their immediate reaction was, "Now you have gone too far!" The old-style sales training that the customer is always right was more than just training, it was a mantra! It was repeated over and over as a formula that represented a truism. The paradigm shift to understanding that the client is not always right is easy to make when you use safety as the catalyst.

An easy example was viewed at an RV dealership when a client pulled up driving a mini SUV towing a twenty-foot travel trailer. After looking up the trailer and finding that it weighs 2,300 pounds, it was confirmed that the mini SUV had a towing capacity of 2,400 pounds and could tow the trailer. The problem was once the client filled all the tanks and loaded all their gear, the trailer was too heavy. To make matters worse, the client was looking to trade in a 2,300-pound trailer for an 8,000-pound trailer with the belief that his mini SUV could tow any twenty-foot trailer. These clients were not right. If the salesperson or dealership did not correct them, the clients could have gotten themselves hurt.

Who teaches such bad advice? To start with, the media does a swell job showing that a standard equipped half-ton pick-up can tow a space shuttle. This is incredibly deceptive because that vehicle can't tow a 16,000-pound fifth-wheel. In fact most of them are only rated to tow 10,000 pounds. The media makes products memorable with such ads but where are they when it comes to safety? Maybe they know that the average truck buyer will never have the opportunity to tow a space shuttle so it takes them off the hook.

What about the refrigerator salesperson who doesn't correct the client who measured their space between cabinets and when the client said it would fit, the salesperson didn't correct them and made the sale. Later when the product is delivered, the door hinges on the top did not fit under the cabinets, and the doors in their open position hit the side wall and other cabinets. Letting this client believe that they are right will lead to poor customer service, heat at the delivery, and will never get you any repeat or referral business.

As specifications and technology continue to change at a staggering pace, it is impossible for your client to keep up with every new way products are being manufactured. It seems that by the time factories get their brochures published and printed, they are already out of date. It is not just the equipment that is making all the changes, it's also the cost of production. Labor, being the most expensive ingredient in most manufacturing, has skyrocketed. Between the minimum wage increases, health care benefit changes, and increases in payroll taxes, the manufactures can't know what their costs will be with the next production schedule. And finally how about the unpredictability of fuel costs?

Now transfer all of these unknown costs to the retailer, who still has to forecast inventory levels based on future sales in an unsure market. What does all of this mean to a customer who is always right? If the factories and the retailers don't know what their true costs are until the end of a fiscal year, how is it that customers always know what the retailer's costs are and what profit margin they should hold? Of course, the client is not always right!

As a professional salesperson, it is your responsibility to correct a client when they are putting themselves in harm's way through educating them on the product. You also owe it to your client to help select the right product for their use based on their needs and budget, and not just the one they saw in an advertisement.

Putting The Client Is Not Always Right Principle to Work

The following questions are designed to gain a working understanding and real application in your business and in your life. Always try to answer the following questions before moving on to the next principle. This will provide you the opportunity to reflect on the value of each principle as a standalone concept. The more quality effort you apply to your answers, the better chance you will see immediate and lasting results from the value of each principle. The questions below are the same at the end of each chapter. Being cognizant of this will allow you to develop an action plan for putting the principles to work as you continue to read.

Define the key points of this principle that you will apply in your business.

Give an example of how the author demonstrated the principle.

Write three real examples of what you would say to your clients to show how you can apply this principle in your business.

Define three plans to exemplify ways that this principle will increase the quality of your selling process, margins, volume, and relationship with your clients.

Write an analogy of how this principle would apply outside of business.

THIRTY-FOUR

HEARING WITHOUT LISTENING

34

Hearing Without Listening

Really listen with your eyes and ears.

"People hearing without listening" is part of the Simon and Garfunkel lyric from the song The Sound of Silence.[10] This is a powerful line for salespeople that begs the question of are we really listening to what our clients are saying? Furthermore, are the questions we are asking meaningful to our clients? And do we just ask the questions because they are part of our selling process or do we really believe in and comprehend what we are asking? And finally, do we really care about the answers to the questions, or are we just getting the answers that our manager said we need?

Ask yourself: Do you care enough to really listen to your client's needs and not just what you think you need to make the sale? Listening to your client will give you all the information you need to help them purchase your product while providing personalized service. To enhance your ability, think of the

---

10   Simon & Garfunkel. *The Sound of Silence*. Tom Wilson, 1965. Vinyl recording.

principle "Start with an Empty Head." Clear your mind of all past clients and listen to what the client in front of you is saying. Don't jump to any conclusions until you have heard all of the information that is important to your client.

A motorcycle dealer's experience that exemplifies this principle was when two ladies wanted to purchase matching motorcycles. The dealer had a white one and an orange one in stock. One of the ladies said the white was exactly what she wanted, while the other said she didn't like white or orange. When other colors were offered, she said none would work. While she sounded like she didn't want a bike right now, she was still there at the business. Her friend purchased the white bike and was urging the other friend to purchase the orange one so she could have a riding partner. After sitting down with the friend, it turned out that she had credit challenges that were keeping her from joining her friend in the purchase that day. Once this was on the table, the client who purchased the white one also purchased the orange one and set up a plan for her friend to pay her back.

Another example from the same business came when a client was prejudged to be able to afford the nicest product in stock. The salesperson promptly gave the best presentation the client has ever seen. This all would have been great, but the salesperson failed to hear that the client was planning on taking the product off-road. The nicest product was a street-only bike and would not work properly off-road. Luckily, one of the managers got involved and started listening to the client's needs, not just their budget. Once the client was shown an off-road product, the purchasing decision came fast.

How many sales we lose by not really listening is a question that no manager or owner ever wants to know the answer to. The best idea of the real loss would be to compare your top salesperson's productivity to that of your bottom salesperson. If you are the salesperson at the bottom, please use this chapter to motivate yourself to be a better listener. Listen because you care, listen because you want to provide the best service, listen because you need the information to select the right product for your client, listen because it is part of your selling process, listen because you believe it is the only way to help your client, and finally, listen because it is your job!

Another way to listen is with your eyes. For years, in class, students have been asked if clients listen more with their eyes or with their ears. The answer is always the same. The eyes have it! Since our clients listen more with their eyes, it only makes sense that we learn to communicate correctly to what our clients are seeing. When a client sees information and says what they saw, it was the client who said it first and thus, their idea.

"Have you ever been driving and, at an unexpected time, come upon traffic while going 60 miles per hour and had to come to a quick stop? What is the first thing you do (make a quick hand gesture like you are pushing down on the brake)?" If you say this, you can expect your client to respond by saying that they jam on, or hit the brake. Their response is directly related to what you did, not what you said. Without the hand gesture, the client may have said that they gently feather the brake in rapid equal sequential intervals knowing that the brakes work better this way. You would have missed the opportunity to explain how anti-lock brakes will solve the client's needs when they find the need to stop quickly.

Speaking to a client's eyes is as important as listening with your eyes. Long before your client speaks, you are judging their response to what you are saying by their physical reaction. Many times you will find yourself changing what you are saying to change how they are physically responding. Study how your clients are reacting to what you are saying. Try to continuously find better ways to present your information in ways that have measurable results.

Care enough to really listen!

Putting The Hearing Without Listening Principle to Work

The following questions are designed to gain a working understanding and real application in your business and in your life. Always try to answer the following questions before moving on to the next principle. This will provide you the opportunity to reflect on the value of each principle as a standalone concept. The more quality effort you apply to your answers, the better chance you will see immediate and lasting results from the value of each principle. The questions below are the same at the end of each chapter. Being cognizant of this will allow you to develop an action plan for putting the principles to work as you continue to read.

Define the key points of this principle that you will apply in your business.

Give an example of how the author demonstrated the principle.

Write three real examples of what you would say to your clients to show how you can apply this principle in your business.

Define three plans to exemplify ways that this principle will increase the quality of your selling process, margins, volume, and relationship with your clients.

Write an analogy of how this principle would apply outside of business.

THIRTY-FIVE

PLAY TO WIN

Do you know people who have the goal of not losing? When they play golf in a foursome their goal is not to be fourth, but to them second or third is acceptable. This striving to not be the worst is not what this principle is about. Many salespeople strive to not be on the bottom of the sales board where they may be in jeopardy of losing their jobs, while top salespeople play to win! If not losing is your goal, you will rarely win. Your winning will come when the top producers get injured, or take time off. It will not be recognized as a true victory by anyone who counts, including yourself.

This chapter is about playing to win as your only goal. It means that you are prepared to do whatever it takes in the weight room to be strong enough and fast enough to achieve the victory. It means you will do more than the competition in studying your product, learning inventory, practicing sales skills, role-playing, and put in whatever hours it takes to end up on top.

When others talk about top producers, they have often said, "I wonder how good that person really is? He will always beat the person who comes in second, but what if he played to his own capabilities?" There was a top salesperson named Bill who set his goal to beat Frank, the number two producer. If Frank sold 20, Bill sold 22. When Frank sold 25, Bill did what he needed to sell 26. The question is not just how good would Bill be without Frank, but if Frank never existed, how good would Bill be?

If you are a top producer, play to your game plan. In college football, there are some teams who appear to run up the score as if to demoralize their competition or to get a higher national ranking. This is not always the case. These top scoring teams sometimes pull their starters out in the first half and their replacements continue to execute just as well. The second and even third string players play to the same game plan and if it is effective, it can't be stopped. You would not and should not expect winning teams to practice plays that won't work so the competition would look better, or not feel so bad. The same holds true in sales. Can you imagine a sales manager pulling their top salesperson aside and telling them to slow down because they are making all the other salespeople feel bad?

Salesperson of the month may be the
top producer's short-term goal,
but they really want the championship
-- salesperson of the year --
year after year!

In a Sobel University pullout course with top producers from all over the United States and Canada, the question of how many hours do you work in a week was asked of the group and everyone answered and heard the others' answers. The top two salespeople were scheduled to answer last. As the numbers were being said, the top salesperson was fidgeting in his chair and saying under his breath that the numbers were coming in too low. Most salespeople were saying between 45-55 hours per week and that they would stay late or come in on their day off to not miss a sales commission. When it came time for the number one salesperson to talk, he said that he never worked less than 60 hours per week. He said that he is always the first in and the last to leave. He did his side work, studying and follow-up before others even arrived.

The number two salesperson who was $50,000 behind the top salesperson, and $50,000 ahead of most of the others, was concerned about the hours that the top person ahead of him was working. The number two wanted the income of the number one, but had different goals in his time off and was concerned about jumping his working hours from 45 to 60-plus hours per week and what effect it would have on his quality home life. Later his concerns were put to rest when he learned that he was already working more hours. The top salesperson was taking two to three months off per year and making up for the time off by working more hours when he did work. The number two salesperson saw this and understood that he still had the opportunity to increase his income by working smarter.

When you play to win, and you do win, there is typically a burst of emotion at that moment of victory that has been kept in check while you were intensely focusing on the job at hand. The easiest example of this is watching a star professional basketball player just after they win their championship. They jump in the air while pumping their fist, collapse to the hardwood and often times you can observe them fighting back their tears. This uncontrollable emotional release comes from an intense focus and exertion to win. When you win, it is necessary that you celebrate your victory. You've earned it!

After the victory celebration, it is amazing to watch the championship players quickly get their game faces back on. Sometimes, ten minutes after the player was sobbing on the floor, they are interviewed on national TV. Their game face is back on as they say, "This championship took a lot of work. The competition was fierce. They will be ready for us next year so we will need to up our game to be able to win again." The victory is already stored and the work for the next game has already begun. When you play to win and the celebration is over, it's back to work. Top sales professionals don't celebrate too long or they miss the next selling opportunity.

Later in this book, other chapters will help identify what top salespeople do to stay on top. The principles titled Be Ready and Go To Work To Work will deliver more information about how and why winners win.

Putting The Play to Win
Principle to Work

The following questions are designed to gain a working understanding and real application in your business and in your life. Always try to answer the following questions before moving on to the next principle. This will provide you the opportunity to reflect on the value of each principle as a standalone concept. The more quality effort you apply to your answers, the better chance you will see immediate and lasting results from the value of each principle. The questions below are the same at the end of each chapter. Being cognizant of this will allow you to develop an action plan for putting the principles to work as you continue to read.

Define the key points of this principle that you will apply in your business.

Give an example of how the author demonstrated the principle.

Write three real examples of what you would say to your clients to show how you can apply this principle in your business.

Define three plans to exemplify ways that this principle will increase the quality of your selling process, margins, volume, and relationship with your clients.

Write an analogy of how this principle would apply outside of business.

THIRTY-SIX

PASSION FOR LEARNING

Do you love to learn? Do you crave learning as much as your favorite dessert? If you do, you may be an Epiphany Junkie. This instant state of amazement, or 'oh wow' moment, is instant stimulation and candy for your brain. Once you get hooked on the joys of learning, you will crave epiphanies and search for them daily.

A business owner expressed that he learns one new thing per day, and has for years. He went on to explain that it couldn't be something that he scheduled to learn like a new word he could read in the dictionary. The new thing had to find him. This is tough. Try it for 30 days. You will find that you will have to change the way you see the world to let new information be revealed.

How you see the world could start first thing in the morning, with your daily commute to work. You may have to drive to work a different way for the opportunity to see and learn something new. When you open your mind on your way to work, you will be ready for your next client more quickly. Try to stretch out your mind before your daily work. It is the same as stretching any muscle before exercise.

Learning can come from many sources. Learn from your last sale, the one you lost, the one the other salesperson just made. Learn from reading, watching and listening. Learn from mentors, managers, and people who have walked the same path before you. Be open to learn from anyone and anywhere. There are messages being delivered all around you all day long. To be open to receive new information, you must keep your desire to share what you know in check, so you can focus on listening and learning.

This principle, Passion For Learning, is all about the word passion. Some other words for passion in this context include: strong emotion, affection, dedication, devotion, eagerness, fire, and excitement. There are many more than these words that are used to define passion, but they all include feelings of action with intense energy and focus toward the goal. And in this case it is learning!

Are you excited to learn and eager to share what you have learned with your clients? This love of knowledge is contagious. Your clients will see and feel the excitement you bring as you deliver the new information. The energy will be an unmeasured and unexpected catalyst toward a positive purchasing decision.

Putting The Passion For Learning Principle to Work

The following questions are designed to gain a working understanding and real application in your business and in your life. Always try to answer the following questions before moving on to the next principle. This will provide you the opportunity to reflect on the value of each principle as a standalone concept. The more quality effort you apply to your answers, the better chance you will see immediate and lasting results from the value of each principle. The questions below are the same at the end of each chapter. Being cognizant of this will allow you to develop an action plan for putting the principles to work as you continue to read.

Define the key points of this principle that you will apply in your business.

Give an example of how the author demonstrated the principle.

Write three real examples of what you would say to your clients to show how you can apply this principle in your business.

Define three plans to exemplify ways that this principle will increase the quality of your selling process, margins, volume, and relationship with your clients.

Write an analogy of how this principle would apply outside of business.

THIRTY-SEVEN

SPAN OF CONTROL

WHAT IS THE COST TO YOUR BUSINESS?

Span of Control refers to the number of units, tasks, projects, or people that can be managed effectively at one time by the same person. When we take on too much, although the work may get completed, the quality could suffer. We justify our busy schedules by saying to ourselves, "I can add one more thing to my plate," or "If you want something done give it to a busy person. They always get things done." As our economy is forever changing, we are challenged by this Span of Control in all areas of our business.

Let's start with how Span of Control can affect salespeople. Picture a January day in central Canada and looking outside at the temperature posted on the bank sign across the street and seeing 40 degrees below zero. As you look to the front door, you see clients coming in from the snow and asking to see a travel trailer. You would think, "Now this is a serious customer to come out in this freezing temperature. They

195

must be ready to buy!" After further study, we found that the salespeople in this dealership had an eighty percent closing ratio in the winter and yet these same salespeople could not average a ten percent closing ratio in the summer. Would this correlation confirm the theory about customers being more serious in the winter?

It was not that simple. Applying the Span of Control Principle, the salespeople had less on their plate in the winter, allowing for a drastic increase in the quality of their work. In the winter, at forty below zero, this one customer may be the only one this week. Knowing this, the salespeople give their absolute best presentation and are prepared to spend all day with one customer. As they believe they may not get another customer all week, they don't accept losing the sale as an option, they handle more objections and provide the best level of service they know how to give. All of this leads to a high closing ratio with a high level of customer satisfaction.

So what happens in the summer? Those same salespeople who know the value of a customer coming through their door in the winter have a different job in the summer. Instead of talking to one customer in a week, they may talk to three to five in a single day. This leads to the all-important question of how many customers can we give an A+ presentation to in a day? Also, what is the consequence of anything less than an A+ presentation? And finally, how long does it take to give an A+ presentation?

Picture this: You are fifteen minutes into delivering your best presentation, and your customer's phone rings. They learn that there is a family situation that requires that they leave now! The question is when they get their family situation under control, will they come back to you or will they say, "We saw what he had, let's go see what the other guy has to offer." If Span of Control limits you from giving your best A+ presentation, the customer is not likely to return.

When asking top sales professionals how long it takes to give their best presentation from meet and greet to closing the sale, the answer is always between two and five hours. The question that follows is very revealing: "If it takes three hours to give your best presentation and sell a product, how many presentations can you give in a day while still having the time to do your side work, another delivery, follow-up other customers properly and handle other daily activities?" Most top salespeople confess that they can handle two new customer presentations per day at the A+ level with everything else they must complete in that same day. When salespeople are forced to handle too many customers, some get forgotten or the quality of service is compromised. If this goes on for too long it becomes your sales culture, and then an enormous long-term expense to your business.

At the salesperson level, as the economy recovers and more customers are returning to our businesses, we must be staffed to maintain the quality of our presentations. This also is true in sales management. Over the past few years, there has been more downsizing in sales management than in the previous ten years combined. Many business owners are running their entire business themselves when before they had a general manager as well as a sales manager. While they have the capacity to get the job done, what about the quality?

When business owners cut expenses in sales management thinking they will save money, they may be putting in place a whole new set of challenges. The examples listed below all have drastic consequences when you examine how your customers view your business and their propensity to return to your business in the future. All of the examples have been recently viewed at businesses and by quality people who, because of Span of Control challenges, have compromised what they know to be their best quality work.

THE LIST GOES AS FOLLOWS:

- Managers are not holding daily time management meetings to schedule their day and sync it with their employees.

- Productivity and lost opportunities are not being measured, and strategies for remediation are not being addressed.

- Daily product training is not being done; quality to our customers is dropping.

- Sales training techniques being used are becoming dated and ineffective.

- Correct staffing has been compromised. We are knowingly allowing our customers to receive a B or C presentation.

- We are keeping employees that are not productive for too long because we know that we do not have the time to train them and can't hold them accountable without the skills.

- Training to develop employees has been dropped or cut to a nonproductive level.

- Employee notices and behavior changes that are needed have been traded with, "It's not worth the fight," or, "I am willing to be held hostage" because we are too busy just trying to get everything else done.

- Standard levels of production have dropped because everyone has too much on their plate.

- "That's good enough" has replaced "Thank you for your hard and quality work."

- "Since there is no time to do the job well, I'm just doing this job for the money - - I really don't care about the people, the customers, or the business" attitude must not be in your business!

One can't believe that business owners have stopped caring about their people or value them any less today. What is known to be quality has been traded for survival over economic downturns for some businesses on the fence. To get back to being on the offense in developing your business, you must first address your Span of Control. Work done at a higher level of quality will be your way out of any tough economic times. Systems you put in place will guarantee a minimum level of productivity while allowing the top producers to have no limit. Customers must be valued, respected, and be given an A+ presentation on every visit. Even if they do not buy today, if they received the best service at your business they will tell others, and may be back. We must care enough to never let a customer leave unhappy, as stated in Chapter Twenty Two.

What's being suggested with this principle is that you correct your Span of Control and increase your productivity in all areas of professional sales. No one will say that this will be easy. Rather that it will be required for you to build your client base with a strong foundation to withstand whatever will be coming at you next. Last, put in systems, controls, and organizational tools that take the place of guessing what should be done or settling for doing a job at a level that you know is less than your best.

Putting The Span of Control Principle to Work

The following questions are designed to gain a working understanding and real application in your business and in your life. Always try to answer the following questions before moving on to the next principle. This will provide you the opportunity to reflect on the value of each principle as a standalone concept. The more quality effort you apply to your answers, the better chance you will see immediate and lasting results from the value of each principle. The questions below are the same at the end of each chapter. Being cognizant of this will allow you to develop an action plan for putting the principles to work as you continue to read.

Define the key points of this principle that you will apply in your business.

Give an example of how the author demonstrated the principle.

Write three real examples of what you would say to your clients to show how you can apply this principle in your business.

Define three plans to exemplify ways that this principle will increase the quality of your selling process, margins, volume, and relationship with your clients.

Write an analogy of how this principle would apply outside of business.

THIRTY-EIGHT

Systems

Having a set of principles that guides our behavior is at the core of any good selling system. Systems are just a combination of parts that come together in a specific order that creates a single directed pathway. When you set up your system, or go to work in an established system, be sure that you believe in and understand all of the system's parts. If you choose not to execute a part of the system, the whole system will break down. For example, if you skip step two (which may be your product selection step) in your selling system, then all the steps that follow may be taken off course with no planned direction.

Businesses rely on Systems because they guarantee a minimum level of productivity. If all salespeople follow the same steps in their selling process, you can measure results. While Systems guarantee a minimum level of productivity, good systems have unlimited upward potential.

As a sales training company for more than two decades, the reason that businesses request training has changed drastically over time. It used to be that businesses just wanted techniques that would increase their sales immediately. This has not been the case for at least the last ten years. The first request we receive from potential clients today is always said the same way: "We need a selling system."

Why did it take until recently for most sales organizations to realize that they needed a selling system? First, let's address the fears of a system. Selling systems expose problem areas in your business, and the old salespeople would fight to have themselves stay under the radar where they are safe from being measured. The three areas that Systems aggressively address are: accountability, measurable results, and systems require a certain level of work. While none of these are bad things in a business, there is no place for a below average salesperson to hide.

Good selling systems identify problems areas quickly, causing instant accountability. They do so by offering a productive way of accomplishing a selling step. At Sobel University, new salespeople frequently say, "I wish someone would have taught me this twenty years ago." Once a new productive system or step in the sale is laid out and it makes perfect sense, it is impossible to go back.

Once the track has been laid, it is time to measure the results. This word accountability should not be scary. It simply means that you want to isolate problem areas for remediation.

This word remediation simply means to actively fix or remove something that is nonproductive or ineffective. Top salespeople are always looking to get better. They want to identify the reason they lost the last sale and correct the problem before they speak to the next client. Unfortunately, the bottom salespeople are filling their time with filibusters and long orations to avoid being exposed for their problem areas. This not wanting to be exposed can keep a business from growing or even simply surviving in the tough economy.

For accountability to work, there must be no negative talk when isolating problem areas. For example, when a salesperson has a low closing ratio, there is no need to beat them down. Rather, you should congratulate them for logging all of their sales opportunities so you can find the best way to help them succeed. Too often the negative words are spoken about the low closing ratio and the salesperson fixes the problem by not logging all of the lost sales. Now you don't know that there is a problem, so you can't fix it. Accountability should have a positive spin because it identifies areas to fix for a pay raise.

The next area that Systems address is measurable results. If your go-to closing technique is a summary close, and you use it with a cash buyer and ask them what they feel comfortable paying after you summarize the benefits of the product, you will often get an offer that is lower than the total price. In this case, your profit margins, which are measured, will be identified as lower than they should be and you can go back and change your closing method. By having a consistent selling system you can better measure, identify and set an action plan to fix problems before the cost is losing a good team member.

Last, Systems require a certain level of work. The only additional effort that a system requires is the initial change. Surprisingly, this usually is just learning new sales word tracks to help you do a better job at what you are already doing. You could find that you are spending more time fixing the problems of an old word track than the time it would take to learn what is new and more productive.

One example is the enormous time salespeople spend trying to close a client on a product that doesn't fit their wants, needs, or budget. If you set up a system that doesn't allow you to show a product until you know the client's wants, needs and budget, and only show what is under their budget, you will save on all of that closing time. Your new system will not just save time, but be less stressful for you and your client.

As mentioned, the initial change will require additional work; the rest of the work should be a trade with what you are doing currently. Daily study time to reinforce the behaviors you want in the game, product study, sales technique study, and time to follow-up with clients should already be in place in your selling system. The reason setting up a system could seem to be challenging or insurmountable is because many businesses don't already have the study time in place or even have a selling system.

The opposite of having a selling system is going out and winging it. Clients today will not put up with this and don't have to. In the old days salespeople said whatever they thought they needed to say to gain a sale. Clients are educating themselves on your product and competition before they come to see you.

Your selling system must complement what your clients have already learned and provide what they still need to learn to feel confident in making a purchasing decision.

When you install a selling system, the improvement is instant. Think of how you open the door of your house to go outside. Since the hinges are always on the inside, for safety, you have to take two steps backward to get out of the way of the door as it opens before you can go outside. Putting in a selling system is the way you would enter your house, not leave. When you enter, you unlock the door (use a selling technique) and step inside. There is no need to go backward.

You already have many systems in your life that you probably don't even think about. The way you brush your teeth the same way every time is a system. You do it the same way to be efficient in movement while being productive and not missing any single tooth. In fact, most of your daily routines have your systems stamped all over them.

Systems offer controls that are measurable so that you can pay attention to the details and not the repetitive movements that are simple muscle memory. The details identify the variables in your sales presentations so that you can fix problem areas and stay on track. This staying on track will reduce stress for you and your client.

Putting The Systems Principle to Work

The following questions are designed to gain a working understanding and real application in your business and in your life. Always try to answer the following questions before moving on to the next principle. This will provide you the opportunity to reflect on the value of each principle as a standalone concept. The more quality effort you apply to your answers, the better chance you will see immediate and lasting results from the value of each principle. The questions below are the same at the end of each chapter. Being cognizant of this will allow you to develop an action plan for putting the principles to work as you continue to read.

Define the key points of this principle that you will apply in your business.

Give an example of how the author demonstrated the principle.

Write three real examples of what you would say to your clients to show how you can apply this principle in your business.

Define three plans to exemplify ways that this principle will increase the quality of your selling process, margins, volume, and relationship with your clients.

Write an analogy of how this principle would apply outside of business.

THIRTY-NINE

LISTEN TO YOURSELF

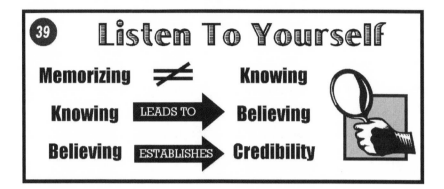

If there is not an expression that has to do with people who speak with nothing intelligible coming out, there should be! Many salespeople take the time to memorize sales presentations yet don't take the time to understand what they are saying. When you say something without understanding what you are saying it is like singing a song with the words not matching up to the music. Pauses are in the wrong place and key words are not expressed correctly. As a presenter, you will not make sense.

To help explain this principle,
follow the equation below:

MEMORIZING does not equal KNOWING

KNOWING leads to BELIEVING

BELIEVING establishes CREDIBILITY

If you take the time to memorize, then take the time to learn what you are saying. When you learn what you are saying you can reach more people if you need to speak in analogy (as in the De-Can Your Presentation Principle). Simple memorization may be what a waiter does at a short-order restaurant. At the higher-end restaurants the waiter has tasted the cuisine and can tell you about how the meal is prepared and about its flavor, not just read the menu back to you. When your client wants to know about your product, they want to know more than what they could read in a brochure or find online. More often than not, reading and presenting your product is not enough; you have to get out there and use your product. Go to where others are using your product to really understand why they purchased, and discover all of your product's real-life applications.

Knowing leads to believing. If you don't really know how something works, how can you be sure it works? Because someone told you? If what you are saying doesn't make sense to you, how can you explain it to make sense to your client? If the waiter says, try this, it's really good, how would they know if they have never tried it themselves?

If you take the time to know your product and presentation you will start believing what you say. When you know what you're talking about, clients will seek out your expertise and word will get out that you are the one to purchase from. Credibility will come from your belief in what you are presenting. When you have credibility, you have earned it for yourself and your clients.

Let's use a difference buyer to make a memorable example. If you don't understand that a difference buyer's primary concern is cash out of pocket out the door, you could ask the correct question and not get the correct answer. By simply asking how much they want to spend, the answer you receive could be $50,000. Even if you ask correctly using anchor points (as explained in the Anchoring Principle) and add the words beside or along with your trade, your memorized word track may not reach the client.

The challenge with this difference buyer is that they only have a certain amount of cash along with their trade. If you and your client are not communicating effectively, the client may think that they are telling you that they have $30,000 and they think that their trade is worth $20,000 making a total of the $50,000 that they say they have. If you ask the Anchoring question the following way, you may have less confusion. "So we don't waste your time showing you the wrong product, besides your trade where were you thinking you wanted to start looking $100,000 to $120,000, $120,000 to $150,000, along with your trade $200,000, $300,000?" When the client answers by saying $50,000, you could confirm by holding a pen and saying that you have your trade, the pen, and hold a piece of paper and say, the paper is the $50,000? By knowing what you mean, and listening to what you are saying, it will be easier to understand and clarify your client's responses.

One of the hardest things for a salesperson to understand in this principle is that no one is just like you. You have to prepare your presentations for the target buyer. Since many salespeople never use or purchase the products they sell, preparing your words must be for how your buyer would like to hear the presentation. Deliberate salespeople have a particularly difficult time with this concept. Being deliberate means that you never feel like you have all the facts, and making a purchasing decision is very difficult. If you believe that others are like you, you may talk past the close by wanting to keep giving facts or asking if a client wants to think it over (because that is what you would do).

Listen to yourself and then listen to how your client is reacting and answering what you are communicating. Remember that your clients have a goal when they come to your business. They came to buy and use your product to increase the quality of their life. Try to help them achieve their goals.

Putting The Listen to Yourself
Principle to Work

The following questions are designed to gain a working understanding and real application in your business and in your life. Always try to answer the following questions before moving on to the next principle. This will provide you the opportunity to reflect on the value of each principle as a standalone concept. The more quality effort you apply to your answers, the better chance you will see immediate and lasting results from the value of each principle. The questions below are the same at the end of each chapter. Being cognizant of this will allow you to develop an action plan for putting the principles to work as you continue to read.

Define the key points of this principle that you will apply in your business.

Give an example of how the author demonstrated the principle.

Write three real examples of what you would say to your clients to show how you can apply this principle in your business.

Define three plans to exemplify ways that this principle will increase the quality of your selling process, margins, volume, and relationship with your clients.

Write an analogy of how this principle would apply outside of business.

213

FORTY

EXECUTE

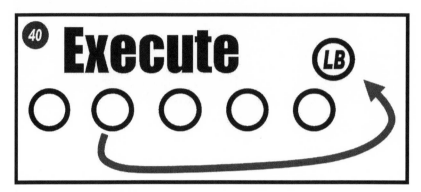

During an interview on a television sports channel, an offensive lineman was telling the story about how his coach in a post-game locker room meeting blamed him for the loss of the last three games. At first, from his story you had to be expecting the losses came from the lineman not protecting the quarterback, but this was not specifically the case. The coach explained that the guard's job was to pull around to the right and knock the linebacker on his butt. Not just block the first defender he saw, not just block the linebacker, but knock the linebacker on his butt and keep him down and unable to rejoin the play until the whistle was blown and the play was over.

The coach grabbed some chalk and started drawing X's and O's on the board. He showed, through illustrations, that if the guard blocked any other player but the linebacker he was effectively changing his teammates' assignments and leaving the linebacker free to break down the play. Once the offensive guard was able to understand the reason the play was drawn out like it was, he was able to let the other defenders by and go straight to the linebacker. Now the whole play was able to work because one player executed his assignment correctly.

To make this translate to sales, we will use Anchoring in the Product Selection step in two different ways. First, if you simply ask, "How much do you want to pay?" Or ask, "How much do you want to spend?" The answers you will receive could be, "As little as possible," "I don't know yet," or "It depends on the product." None of these answers would be effective in helping you select the right product that will come in under the client's budget.

Second, how about if you have products from $50,000 to $100,000 in your inventory available that will fit the client's needs and you ask, "How much did you want to spend today, $10,000 to $20,000?" This would be the same as asking, "Were you thinking you wanted to put down 10%?"

Both of the above examples do not effectively get you the correct answers that you need to serve the client correctly. Asking how much someone wishes to pay, or using a low number or percentage, will not get you into a position to show what you have available in your inventory today.

Because your manager is not with you when you ask these questions, the manager may assume that you asked correctly. Experienced and well-trained managers don't ask salespeople what their customers' answers are; rather they ask how the question was presented and then evaluate the answer.

A better way to execute the above question, taking into account that the client wants to pay cash and your available inventory, would sound like this, "So we don't waste your time showing you the wrong products, where did you want to start looking today, $100,000 to $120,000, $120,000 to $150,000?" This question protects your client's right to see the nicest product their money can buy.

The above correct question also allows your manager and other sales associates to know where you are and be able to help you if needed. If the manager needs to speak directly with your client, the manager will know what you said and can reinforce the information already presented. Without knowing what you said or if what you said was incorrect, the manager could have to start all over with the client. Your clients are paying you to execute the play so that they can purchase your product.

One other example came from a retired professional running back. He said that his coach had the team execute the same running play hundreds of times before we could expect to see it in a game. He explained that the play had to be locked into each player's muscle memory so that in the game, they were watching how the defense reacted rather than thinking of what they were going to do next. At game speed, he explained, there is no time to think. You have to rely on the quality of your practice.

The game of sales is exactly the same. If you practice at game speed and understand the play, you will execute your sales presentation effectively. All variables will be exposed in practice and accounted for. Through critical repetition and muscle memory, you will be able to see what is coming and be prepared. The job of sales is just a game that requires each word track be executed correctly to be able to advance down the field to your goal.

Putting The Execute Principle to Work

The following questions are designed to gain a working understanding and real application in your business and in your life. Always try to answer the following questions before moving on to the next principle. This will provide you the opportunity to reflect on the value of each principle as a standalone concept. The more quality effort you apply to your answers, the better chance you will see immediate and lasting results from the value of each principle. The questions below are the same at the end of each chapter. Being cognizant of this will allow you to develop an action plan for putting the principles to work as you continue to read.

Define the key points of this principle that you will apply in your business.

Give an example of how the author demonstrated the principle.

Write three real examples of what you would say to your clients to show how you can apply this principle in your business.

Define three plans to exemplify ways that this principle will increase the quality of your selling process, margins, volume, and relationship with your clients.

Write an analogy of how this principle would apply outside of business.

FORTY-ONE

SELF-FULFILLING PROPHECY

---

④ SELF-FULFILLING PROPHECY

When you think your client isn't going to buy...
you're right!

Self-Fulfilling Prophecy occurs when what you already believe to know is the confirmed result. The second you believe that your client will not buy today, do you change your presentation? After all, why put in all of the effort that is needed to make a sale if the client will not buy anyway? There are many problems with this type of thinking.

Since you already know that your client will not purchase, your actions will make this your reality. When you know your client will not purchase, you will short cut your presentation, not present the product correctly or completely and never ask for the order. Your outcome is predetermined by your actions; you have self-fulfilled your expectations.

If you quiz any of the experienced salespeople, they will all have a story about when they prejudged a client and how it cost them a sale. One such story is about a salesperson who arrived at work and found that a homeless man was sleeping at the front door. Being alone, the salesperson walked by quietly and went in and locked the door behind him. The lock sound woke the sleeping man and he announced that he wanted to purchase one of the salesperson's products. The salesperson replied through the locked glass door, "We are not open," and walked away. All the salesperson could think about was the smell of the man, his ripped up clothes, dirty beard and big rubber boots.

Yes, the boots were the clue that the salesperson missed. This client was an Alaskan fisherman who had just come off a boat earlier that morning with a boot full of cash, literally! The next salesperson to come to the door, without prejudgment, easily sold the client a product. The next day when the client came back to pick it up, he was dressed in a suit and was cleanly shaven, hardly recognizable from the day before. When you think your client will not purchase, you're right. How much will this cost you?

Recently, an older man with a hip problem and a limp was observed trying to get a salesperson to sell him a motorcycle. Judging the man's physical limitations, no one wanted to help him on a busy Saturday. They all knew that he couldn't handle the bikes they sold, and they didn't want to miss the opportunity with other qualified buyers. Finally, the manager became free and greeted the gentleman. The client quickly said what he wanted and the manager had to empty his head to not prejudge. The man wanted a bike for fun and was sure he could handle it.

The manager took him to a bike with a standard seat height and supported the bike so the client could get on and off. The client quickly realized that getting what he thought he wanted was not a safe possibility. The manager, after changing the client's expectations, then showed a bike with a side-car. The client was thrilled! He didn't have to hold it up or support it when stopped at intersections. It was an easy purchasing decision for the client.

It is unfortunate that these stories exist. Salespeople lose out on commissions, and clients don't get to purchase what they want. Everyone loses. To make a change, it is as easy as changing your Self-Fulfilling Prophecy. Instead of prejudging a client's ability to purchase, believe that there is always another way to help the client get what they want. It has been said that the mother of invention is need. When you need to make a sale, you will find a way. Luckily for you, every client coming to your business has already decided they want to purchase your product. It really is that easy, if that is what you truly believe. This Self-Fulfilling Prophecy is about how what you believe becomes your reality.

If you have been in sales for any length of time you have heard clients say, "We had no intention of purchasing today." Then they meet a salesperson who holds the belief that there is no way the two clients would have driven one hour to get to their business, given up a valuable day off, and not already spent time shopping online unless the clients had the intention of making a purchasing decision. The salesperson's new self-fulfilling prophecy is set, and the client will be purchasing today.

Putting The Self-Fulfilling Prophecy Principle to Work

The following questions are designed to gain a working understanding and real application in your business and in your life. Always try to answer the following questions before moving on to the next principle. This will provide you the opportunity to reflect on the value of each principle as a standalone concept. The more quality effort you apply to your answers, the better chance you will see immediate and lasting results from the value of each principle. The questions below are the same at the end of each chapter. Being cognizant of this will allow you to develop an action plan for putting the principles to work as you continue to read.

Define the key points of this principle that you will apply in your business.

Give an example of how the author demonstrated the principle.

Write three real examples of what you would say to your clients to show how you can apply this principle in your business.

Define three plans to exemplify ways that this principle will increase the quality of your selling process, margins, volume, and relationship with your clients.

Write an analogy of how this principle would apply outside of business.

FORTY-TWO

BE BACK

When Your Client Leaves
You Are Turning Them To The Next Business

This principle was named for all of the clients who leave without purchasing with the final words, "We'll be back." In your business do you track your closing ratio? Of course you do, but do you track your bring back percentage? In almost all businesses that track both numbers, the closing ratio is more than double the bring back ratio. In real numbers if you have a 20% closing ratio, you would bring back less than a 10%.

The numbers first tell us that if you know you are probably not going to bring back clients, you need to help them buy while they are with you now. To be able to close the sale on the clients' first visit to your business, you must give the best presentation that they have ever had in their life. Better than what they feel they can get by continuing to shop. You also must be prepared to turn your client over to another salesperson or manager so they can provide more and new information that will help the client make the decision to buy now.

Turning a client may feel, at first, like you are adding unnecessary pressure, but it is just another technique designed to help the client. Turning is easy if you believe that your business is the best place for your client's service after the sale. If you let your client leave and purchase from a less qualified business, you are doing them no favors.

Think of turning this way: When your client leaves your business, you are turning them to your competitor. This being said, you are better off turning the client within your business and giving them another chance to buy from what you know is the best place for service before, during, and after the sale. Of course, if you know that you are not already the best, become the best and take away all doubt.

The other challenge that you face when a client leaves is how they will come back (again, if they come back). When and if the client comes back to your business, they will be loaded with all of the information they could find online and in print material. They may have prices from other businesses more than 2,000 miles away. They may have read in a brochure that the product can be built a certain way, but you do not have one of those, and the factory stopped building them after the brochure was published.

Another challenge that will never go away is the aging of inventory. The product that you may have may be one week old in your inventory. Your competition could have inventory that is ten months old in the same model year. While your competition is willing to discount their old inventory, you are competing with product that you should be holding a fair margin on.

This also doesn't include the inventory that your factory sells to businesses for less while they are overstocked. Don't forget the businesses that are going to be closing. They may be selling for less than your cost to avoid the factory buyback rate. Then there are the damaged products that are discounted but not advertised as distressed.

The above list goes on and on. What you should count on is that even if you bring a client back, your commission will be compromised. You may also look bad to your client when you were asking a higher price than they could find by continuing to shop. Unfortunately, your clients don't know what it costs to run a business. They will always want the best deal, not understanding that if you sell for a loss, you will not be there to take care of them after the sale.

It is your responsibility to make the profit you need to be there for your clients, and your personal financial needs. No good will come from not giving your client every opportunity to buy from you today.

Just for fun, one manager would have his new salespeople stand outside the business and read the marquees on the buses that passed by. After some time the manager would come out and look at the list that the new salesperson had written. The signs on the buses listed all of the towns and cities in the area that were the next scheduled stops. The manager pointed out that not one of the bus destinations said "Be Back." The manager then explained to the new salesperson that since the Be Back bus doesn't stop here, we need to close everyone before they leave.

Another sales manager found himself eating three to four free lunches per day as he was betting the salespeople that their clients would not be back. We all would like to believe that our clients really like us and will not buy from anyone else. Think about this, your clients always buy from the last place they shop. If it is not with you, it will be with your competition.

Putting The Be Back Principle to Work

The following questions are designed to gain a working understanding and real application in your business and in your life. Always try to answer the following questions before moving on to the next principle. This will provide you the opportunity to reflect on the value of each principle as a standalone concept. The more quality effort you apply to your answers, the better chance you will see immediate and lasting results from the value of each principle. The questions below are the same at the end of each chapter. Being cognizant of this will allow you to develop an action plan for putting the principles to work as you continue to read.

Define the key points of this principle that you will apply in your business.

Give an example of how the author demonstrated the principle.

Write three real examples of what you would say to your clients to show how you can apply this principle in your business.

Define three plans to exemplify ways that this principle will increase the quality of your selling process, margins, volume, and relationship with your clients.

Write an analogy of how this principle would apply outside of business.

FORTY-THREE

THIRD BASE

The Third Base Principle received its name from not just from any baseball, but from watching women's softball at the college level. If you haven't had the chance to watch this game, you are missing out. It is a fast-paced sport that is played by incredible athletes and coached by incredible tacticians. The unpaid players give their all in every moment of the action. There are a lot of salespeople could learn from watching the focus, training, coaching, routines, preparation, intensity, and pure love of the game. This principle will focus on one aspect from the game: Reflexes versus Reaction.

When the position of shortstop is played, in most cases, the player lines up behind the base line. This gives the player more time to judge the ball as it comes off the bat and takes a bounce or two. It also gives the player the opportunity to move toward the ball with less body twisting and time the pick-up and throw to first base. This, while it happens very fast, still allows the player time to think and react.

The third base position in softball is very different. With all of the slap hitting and bunting the third base position may be played from just thirty feet from home plate. You can even see the third base player charging closer if they suspect a bunt. Now if the batter pulls their bat back and takes a full swing, the third base player has no time to react as the ball is rocketed toward them. This is where the position becomes all about reflexes.

Are these people born with the ability to play this position with lightning fast reflexes, or can you train to develop the skills? If you had the opportunity to watch the University of Washington's ladies softball team in the 2014 season, you would know that it is learned because four different athletes had to be moved from their regular starting position during different parts of the season, and they all did a great job. For you real baseball fans, this was not planned, this was a necessity because of injuries at other positions.

How are reflexes learned? In softball, as in sales, reflexes are developed in the following order:
Reflex comes from,
Critical Repetition, which develops
Muscle Memory, which gives you
Reliability, when needed.

Critical repetition is not just doing the same thing over and over. It is the execution of a motion with meticulous precision. There is very little room for error when the ball is traveling toward your face at more than 100 miles per hour and you are thirty feet from contact. Thousands of balls are hit to only the third base player during practices to develop muscle memory. After all of this practice, the player will develop reliability when called on in the game.

Now you are about to greet your client and they say, "We're just looking." You as a salesperson must now use your reflex training and muscle memory to respond correctly to a client who is sending you the message that they don't want or need your help. You don't have time to think of what to say so you respond with what your training has provided: "So you're just looking, that's great. You probably want an education on what makes, models, and prices we have available? How about we set that as your goal of good service and just give you an education on your visit today?" After your client responds, follow by saying, "So let's get started." After years of critical repetition as a salesperson, you already know that no client will purchase without the proper education on your product. Your reflex in this case just put the client on the right path toward owning your product.

In softball and sales, the time you put in during practice will allow you to perform the way you need to in game situations. Be sure to practice at full speed to be ready for anything that is thrown at you during your sales presentations.

Putting The Third Base
Principle to Work

The following questions are designed to gain a working understanding and real application in your business and in your life. Always try to answer the following questions before moving on to the next principle. This will provide you the opportunity to reflect on the value of each principle as a standalone concept. The more quality effort you apply to your answers, the better chance you will see immediate and lasting results from the value of each principle. The questions below are the same at the end of each chapter. Being cognizant of this will allow you to develop an action plan for putting the principles to work as you continue to read.

Define the key points of this principle that you will apply in your business.

Give an example of how the author demonstrated the principle.

Write three real examples of what you would say to your clients to show how you can apply this principle in your business.

Define three plans to exemplify ways that this principle will increase the quality of your selling process, margins, volume, and relationship with your clients.

Write an analogy of how this principle would apply outside of business.

FORTY-FOUR

DO IT NOW

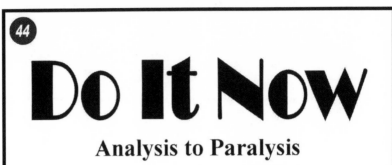

Analysis to Paralysis

There is an old saying, "Don't put off until tomorrow what you can do today." In sales, much of your time is dictated by your clients. You don't always know when they will call or come in to see you. Even on the internet, your client is only there for so long after they type in a question. If you don't respond almost immediately, they may be offline and on to their next task in life. With our clients dictating much of our schedule, we don't have time to put off anything for later. When later comes, we will be busy doing something else and what we set aside gets moved to the bottom of the list. If it wasn't important enough to do already, well, it can still wait.

This type of attitude will not serve you well as a salesperson or a sales manager. It seems in the spring, every year, the same conversation occurs in businesses that sell seasonal products. They hire new salespeople for the season and before they train them properly, the season starts. Now they have untrained salespeople performing below the business's standards, frustrating the other professional salespeople while asking for help, frustrating the managers who are required to give them more time in a sales presentation, and finally, frustrating the clients who want answers to questions that the new, untrained salesperson does not know.

Think about how this frustrates the new salesperson as well. If they are paid on commission and don't have the skills to make enough money to survive the off-season, they have to leave. This sets the chain of events to reload every year. The Do It Now Principle applies to training as well as tasks and activities. If you don't have the time to train properly, you should not be hiring. The cost of an untrained salesperson is immeasurable when you take into account the lost sales and everyone those poorly treated clients tell about their experience.

In a previous principle, the concept of analysis to paralysis was introduced. This is the principle that will be defined by this concept. When you run across a deliberate person who tends to think about a topic so deeply that nothing gets done, you have witnessed analysis to paralysis. Do It Now means that you look at your options, view the research, and then get it done now. It does not mean that you do anything halfway or at a compromised level. It simply means that you do it now. Really, it is that simple.

For our purposes, the word productivity is the measurable rate at which we receive and sell our products. At any link in our receiving and selling process, the Do It Now Principle could have drastic consequences. What if the product is perishable and the new, untrained driver takes a new route for the delivery? What if the manufacturer takes a coffee break and misses the delivery to the boat that only transports once a month? What if a salesperson decides to make their follow-up calls later and then gets busy and can't call? What if the parts manager forgets to order a part and the client shows up to have it installed one month later and it is not there? What if the sales manager puts off their daily training meeting and the skill that was scheduled to be learned was needed for your next client? What if the product side work is not done, and you have to show a product that is not clean or operational?

You get the idea: Do It Now!

Putting The Do It Now
Principle to Work

The following questions are designed to gain a working understanding and real application in your business and in your life. Always try to answer the following questions before moving on to the next principle. This will provide you the opportunity to reflect on the value of each principle as a standalone concept. The more quality effort you apply to your answers, the better chance you will see immediate and lasting results from the value of each principle. The questions below are the same at the end of each chapter. Being cognizant of this will allow you to develop an action plan for putting the principles to work as you continue to read.

Define the key points of this principle that you will apply in your business.

Give an example of how the author demonstrated the principle.

Write three real examples of what you would say to your clients to show how you can apply this principle in your business.

Define three plans to exemplify ways that this principle will increase the quality of your selling process, margins, volume, and relationship with your clients.

Write an analogy of how this principle would apply outside of business.

235

FORTY-FIVE

TRUST

There is a business owner who struggles with getting his workers to a productive level and maintaining the pace. In observing his dealings with salespeople, outside representatives, and even his own managers there is a level of mistrust that you can see in his eyes and hear in his tone. His frustration level at work is always above normal and is noticeable by all who work with him. Even when he has a financially good period, there are excuses and doubts that it will continue. His turnover is high, and it takes a certain kind of person to work with him long term. They must have very strong self-esteem, be used to abuse, or finally many of them have a past that does not allow them to work for other businesses.

This business owner didn't get to this place overnight, and his challenges will continue until he learns how to trust. To learn how to not trust others comes from years of being let down and disappointed in your expectations. Once you get to that point, you become consumed with the belief that you can't trust anyone, and you are setting yourself up in advance for the ultimate letdown. It truly becomes a self-fulfilling prophecy. It is a heavy load to carry, and everyone around you sees your stress and tries to stay out of your way. Thus, attracting good employees and maintaining a working trust relationship is difficult, if not impossible.

The empowerment of others so that they can do their job is difficult for a person who does not trust. In this business, the managers are afraid to make a decision because they already know it will be wrong in their supervisor's eyes and are afraid of losing their jobs. Until training at this place, never before in thirty years as trainers have we been told that the salespeople are not motivated to take the next client. There could be other factors contributing to this. For example, the business is understaffed. However, the lack of staffing goes back to the challenges of working in this business. From the outside looking in, it doesn't appear that anyone is having any fun. In fact, it looks like most everyone is in a constant state of misery, resigned to the fact that anything they do will be wrong.

Proverbs are fascinating because they reveal a known truth though an atypical lens and yet were created anciently or have become unsourceable. In the above business situation, an old proverb comes to mind: "To be trustworthy, you must learn to trust others first." If one believes that all others are not to be trusted, do you think that the business owner above beats them to the punch so he doesn't have to be let down later?

As a business owner, sales manager, or a sales professional, you must trust the people you are working with. If this is not within your comfort zone, start small. Lower your expectations and just get victories. As a business owner, start out by giving small, attainable projects one at a time and then catch the people you gave the jobs to doing something right. Then increase the responsibilities gradually, while maintaining victories. This will do wonders for your employees' self-esteem and confidence in working with you. As you build this trust relationship, you will find that as you learn to trust others, you will in fact become trustworthy yourself.

In time, you may enjoy the benefits that come from trusting others and having them trust you. In training key employees in all positions in your business, you must empower them to make the right decision when you are not present. When you trust your employees, they may just surprise you and come back with better work than you expected. They achieve this when they feel trusted and empowered to be creative. Still, sometimes they miss the mark. In trusting others it is better to miss the mark, learn, and grow, than not do a job because they are afraid of being put down at the end. Continue to build on these victories so that when you are faced with something important, you have a winning method.

Trust at all levels in a business is critical to a salesperson's development and productivity. First, you must trust your selling process. This means that you believe in Principle Three, Selling By Compartments, and you know the importance of Principle Thirty-Eight, Systems. When you trust your process, you will not let a client take you off the correct path. Just as the business owner did not trust his employees and they did not trust him, your clients will feel the same way about you if you do not do what is right with your selling process.

For example, if you skip the step where you sit down and find all the information needed to show the right product, and show the wrong model, you will lose the client's trust if you go to show a second or third model. The loss of Trust is revealed when you have made a client fall in love with a product that is out of their budget. This can never happen if you follow your selling process. Trust that your process has all of the built-in questions and answers needed to help your client make a purchase with no stress and under budget. If you find that your process is not keeping up with the market and builds mistrust, get a new process!

Second, trust your presentation. If you believe in Principle Ten, Interactive Presentation, and Principle Sixteen, Get Permission First, you will have no problem in trusting your presentation. Since your presentation is interactive and educational, it is likely that your client has never been given a presentation this good before. Also, if you are getting permission to go to each further step in your selling process from your client, there can be only a trust relationship. Your presentation should be packed with the principles in this book as each of them exists to help your client purchase.

Third, you must trust your knowledge. This is easy if you know that you have put the time in to learning all there is to know about your product. Salespeople either know they know, or know they don't know their product. There is no gray area here. If you haven't put the time into studying and learning your product and sales presentations, you will not be trustworthy to your clients. If your clients cannot trust that the information that you give them is correct, they will give you poor information in return.

An experienced salesperson was explaining to new salespeople that the "M" engine got its name because it was shaped like an "M." This experienced salesperson went on to say that the new "N" engine got its name because it is shaped like an "N." What is sad is that if this wasn't a true story, it would be comical to that business. The "M" engine was the one built after the "L" engine, and the new "N" engine was built to replace the "M."

Why do some salespeople need to fabricate product knowledge? They know what they are saying is wrong. Is it in fact easier to make up knowledge than to take the time to learn the product? If you are a salesperson who is going to make a conscious choice to represent your business incorrectly then you should do all professional salespeople a favor and leave the industry. This consumer lack of trust that sales professionals face daily comes from the salespeople who earn this lack of trust for the entire sales profession.

Last, you must trust yourself. When you know what you are doing is right for your client and your business, it is easy to show confidence in your presentation. This is not just in your presentation of your product, but in your presentation of yourself to others. Clients want you to be a leader and teacher. If they trust you, they will follow you through the selling process and be happy to request and accept your recommendations. To trust yourself means that you must have had to earn your own trust first. When you look in the mirror, do you see a person who has done all the work to be trustworthy? If you don't see that person yet, get moving.

Putting The Trust Principle to Work

The following questions are designed to gain a working understanding and real application in your business and in your life. Always try to answer the following questions before moving on to the next principle. This will provide you the opportunity to reflect on the value of each principle as a standalone concept. The more quality effort you apply to your answers, the better chance you will see immediate and lasting results from the value of each principle. The questions below are the same at the end of each chapter. Being cognizant of this will allow you to develop an action plan for putting the principles to work as you continue to read.

Define the key points of this principle that you will apply in your business.

Give an example of how the author demonstrated the principle.

Write three real examples of what you would say to your clients to show how you can apply this principle in your business.

Define three plans to exemplify ways that this principle will increase the quality of your selling process, margins, volume, and relationship with your clients.

Write an analogy of how this principle would apply outside of business.

FORTY-SIX

IMMEASURABLE STATISTIC

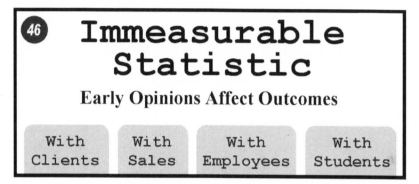

It is an Immeasurable Statistic how many deals we lose because when the client finally realizes we are good people, it is too late in the selling process and they have already sabotaged their deal. Clients lie to us early in the selling process because of the mistrust that they came in with from the last place they shopped. This lying happens throughout the selling process. It happens with clients giving incorrect information to a salesperson. It happens when salespeople lie to themselves about a perception of a client. It happens when a salesperson goes home and shares their day with others. It happens when students attend selling courses. So, it pretty much happens everywhere in and around a sales department.

The first place it happens is when a client lies about their name, phone number or email address. We know this happens because salespeople still make calls to: "You have reached a number that is no longer in service. If you feel this message is in error, please hang up and try your call again."

Why do clients lie so quickly? It may be because you greet the client the same way as the last salesperson: "Welcome to ABC; how may I help you today?" If they left that salesperson without purchasing, the last thing you want to do is remind them of that unpleasant experience. Your meet and greet must be original and all about the client.

Another place in the selling process that a client may lie is when they say they do not have a trade. This comes from all of the people they trust telling them, "Do not tell a salesperson that you have a trade until you negotiate out your best deal. This way if you owe more on your trade than it is worth, the business will have to over allow to get your financing approved." The people these clients are trusting are their credit unions, their parents, and consumer reports. Ironically, none of these people giving the advice planning on purchasing the product for the client. Finding out if a client has a trade is critical in the product selection step if you plan on coming in under budget at the end of your selling process.

The second place we produce an Immeasurable Statistic is when we believe that a client can't buy or we are not creative enough to find a way to make a deal. This happens when we size-up and prejudge our clients based on what they wear, their watch, what they are driving, and sometimes even their grammar. This point was further explained in Chapter Forty-One, Self-Fulfilling Prophecy.

It is immeasurable how many deals we lose because we believe our clients will not purchase. This was recently viewed by watching a timeshare salesperson. He felt that he got an unlucky draw when his clients were already at the highest level in timeshare ownership. They owned more weeks than he had ever seen and could not believe that they would want more. He asked if they had any questions without delivering a presentation on what was new and exciting. He was trying to brush them off as he felt that they were a waste of his time. Finally, the client said how much they loved the timeshare product and asked if they could buy more. This salesperson was lucky that the client wanted the product more than the salesperson wanted to sell it.

The third place we produce an Immeasurable Statistic is when a salesperson goes home and shares their day with the people who care about them. Usually, someone asks if the salesperson sold anything that day. Then the trouble starts. The salesperson, who sold nothing that day, may complain about the clients, their coworkers, their boss, their inventory and their marketing. After hearing this day after day, the family may say to the salesperson that they care about, "If you hate your job that much, you should quit!" It therefore is an Immeasurable Statistic how many salespeople quit the job they love because they have to save face with the ones they care about. If all you share is the bad things that happen in your life, no one will ever want to spend time with you until you make a change.

Another place we produce an Immeasurable Statistic is when we prejudge teachers and managers. If you think that you can't learn anything from the teacher or manager, you are right. You shut your mind down, don't take notes, avoid eye contact with the instructor, and never participate. Worse than that, when you are viewed by the instructor as someone who is only there because you are being made to go, the instructor may give up on you. Unfortunately later when you realize that the instructor's message makes sense and will make you money, it's too late. You have already embarrassed yourself, your coworkers, and your business. You have wasted your business owner's money for the training and made a bold statement that what is important to your business owner is not important to you. It is therefore an Immeasurable Statistic how many salespeople do not take training seriously and do not get the skills needed to make the commission that they deserve.

This principle is about not allowing your client's or your early opinions getting in the way of making a purchase, making a sale, keeping your job, or even having the opportunity for self-improvement. Since you can't set up a statistical test that will measure any of these variables, it is up to you to stay on course.

Putting The Immeasurable Statistic Principle to Work

The following questions are designed to gain a working understanding and real application in your business and in your life. Always try to answer the following questions before moving on to the next principle. This will provide you the opportunity to reflect on the value of each principle as a standalone concept. The more quality effort you apply to your answers, the better chance you will see immediate and lasting results from the value of each principle. The questions below are the same at the end of each chapter. Being cognizant of this will allow you to develop an action plan for putting the principles to work as you continue to read.

Define the key points of this principle that you will apply in your business.

Give an example of how the author demonstrated the principle.

Write three real examples of what you would say to your clients to show how you can apply this principle in your business.

Define three plans to exemplify ways that this principle will increase the quality of your selling process, margins, volume, and relationship with your clients.

Write an analogy of how this principle would apply outside of business.

FORTY-SEVEN
BE ORGANIZED

Many studies have been done on what the number one cause of stress is in the workplace. They all have concluded that it is tied to having a messy desk. A messy desk means that you are in the middle of many projects and can't put any of them away. Projects left unfinished wear on you because it is hard to forget about all you still need to do for one task while you are working on another. Then with so many open projects, clients get forgotten about, orders are not placed and deadlines are not met while you are working on something else. Next you find that you have guilt caused by letting others down, and you take this home with you and never get a break. It becomes easy to see how having a messy desk leads to stress in the workplace.

The Be Organized Principle is an important key to your success as a salesperson or any other position you aspire to. The list below will help you build a case as to why you want to not only be organized, but be seen as organized as well.

- Organized salespeople have higher productivity. They have an organized follow-up system that manages their time so that no client is forgotten about. They schedule their day so that time is not wasted with non-commission moments. They have a set training schedule. They schedule time off to sharpen their saw mentally to be ready when they come back to work. They come to work to work.

- Organized salespeople have reduced stress. They finish one task before starting another. The quality of their work does not require that they have to revisit the same topic again to fix a problem. They have a higher closing ratio and make more money. Their quality of life outside of the business brings no stress to the business.

- Organized salespeople have a better start to their day. Before going home the day before, they completed all open tasks or scheduled them for completion. They come to work to a clean and empty desk. They come in early to get their side work done before clients start showing up and require service. They work out their minds with training every morning. They only wear professional work clothes to work so they see themselves as ready and professional.

- Organized salespeople give off a better perception. Clients never see that a salesperson is too busy to help them. Clients see that this salesperson can get what they need done, and do it now. Clients get a good first impression as the salesperson is clean and well presented.

249

- Organized salespeople attract others. They are the people clients and coworkers go to for answers. They are the people you want to help you. They are the first people chosen for team competition. They always have a smile and are happy to see clients.

- Organized salespeople get more opportunities. They are the first to be considered for promotion. They are the first to be offered a house deal because the owner knows they will give great service and follow through. They are always given the best and most important accounts. They are looked at as role models and leaders.

- Organized salespeople earn trust more quickly. They are transparent in their work so everyone knows what they are doing and thinking at all times. They explain to clients what will happen next. They get permission from their clients on each step in the selling process before proceeding. They follow through so their managers look to them for the answers.

The Be Organized Principle will make your life easier if you are willing to put in the time to set your life to a time management system. Nothing important will be forgotten, the quality of your work and time off will greatly improve, you will become more reliable for yourself and others, and, maybe most important of all, you will greatly reduce stress.

Putting The Be Organized
Principle to Work

The following questions are designed to gain a working understanding and real application in your business and in your life. Always try to answer the following questions before moving on to the next principle. This will provide you the opportunity to reflect on the value of each principle as a standalone concept. The more quality effort you apply to your answers, the better chance you will see immediate and lasting results from the value of each principle. The questions below are the same at the end of each chapter. Being cognizant of this will allow you to develop an action plan for putting the principles to work as you continue to read.

Define the key points of this principle that you will apply in your business.

Give an example of how the author demonstrated the principle.

Write three real examples of what you would say to your clients to show how you can apply this principle in your business.

Define three plans to exemplify ways that this principle will increase the quality of your selling process, margins, volume, and relationship with your clients.

Write an analogy of how this principle would apply outside of business.

FORTY-EIGHT

TOUCH IT ONCE

One of the greatest secrets that productive salespeople know is the Touch It Once Principle. If you take into account getting ready to do something and the cleanup time after, a five minute project could triple in time. For example you need to write a sales order on your computer. Your setup includes getting the information together you need, the ritual in stopping what you are currently doing, turning on your computer (warming it up since it's probably already on), finding and opening the correct file, and thinking about what you want to type. This all took time before you even started doing the actual work.

Now multiply the above time if you don't finish the project the first time it's touched. What about the other distractions that will steal your time while you are working? The phone rings, you answer, and now your thoughts are lost and it takes time to get back on task. While you are on your computer anyway, you check your email or your social media. It is easy for a minute-long project to become an hour of nonproductive time.

The Touch It Once Principle means that you don't start any project that you haven't already scheduled the uninterrupted time to finish. You don't take calls, check your email, or even see what your friends are doing. You focus on the task at hand. When you do this, the quality and quantity of your work will be greatly enhanced. You will quickly find that with your speed and accuracy improving, you will have time to make even more sales.

Another name for this principle could be "scheduled productivity." In this scheduled productivity you not only affect yourself, but others as well. If you are a sales manager who is not prepared for a sales meeting that you are leading, the meeting could run long and thus take your salespeople out of commission. Leaders, managers and salespeople steal time from each other on a daily basis. One person's break can be productive time taken from another. If you have scheduled work, don't let anyone or anything take you off task.

One of the worst time thieves ever invented is email. Ask yourself how many emails are sitting in your inbox currently? Please don't even add what is in your social or promotions inbox. The answers are startling when you consider that most of the email has been opened and looked at more than once. Then, just for fun, think about the email you want to answer that has been your inbox for a week. You may have to scroll through more than fifty other emails and fight off the temptation of looking at them again. Finally, you find what you are looking for and notice that you haven't left enough time to handle the response correctly, so you save it for later once again!

Using email as an example of the Touch It Once Principle is easy. Follow some basic time management rules and you will reclaim hours. First, do not open your email as you go through the day. Many people think that a good time to check email is while they are waiting for a meeting. This may take your head out of the meeting and off task. The meeting may now run long as you try to remember the key points you prepared, or worse, you forget to say something that was important. The old-fashioned walk to a meeting was a good time to review and get focused on the job at hand without any other distractions.

So this first point is to not open any email unless you have scheduled time to complete what you open. This will require that you actually schedule a specific time for email, like from 1 to 1:30 you sit down uninterrupted and get it done. Executives with many projects working at once had to learn this early. If you do too many things at one time the quality suffers and you may not actually get any one thing finished.

Be sure that when you schedule your time for email you don't take yourself out of commission. The time you select should not be when it could be your time to speak to a client. Also, save the personal email for breaks and lunch. There are many commission salespeople who have the discipline to never check their email at work. It's easy. Turn your phone off when you are with a client unless there are sales tools on your phone that you need to help your client.

Saying this is easy is true for those who are not addicted to their phones and their social media. When watching a salesperson get terminated for using their phone instead of focusing on the job, it became evident that this is a true addiction. If you aren't sure if you have this problem, picture leaving your phone home for a day. If this gives you anxiety or stress, then what is the time cost in lost productivity throughout the day for you?

Now that we don't open our email unless we have scheduled time, when you do open it, put the email in one of four categories: Handle it, Schedule it, Print or file it, or Trash it.

• Handle it means that you respond and complete what is needed to finish and close the email. If you can't handle it right now, you have to put it into one of the other categories.

• Schedule it means that you could need other people or information to complete the email. Schedule a specific time for later, when you will have all of the information together, and then will complete the task.

• Print or file it means that you know that you will need this document for reference later. Put it away in a paper or electronic file, labeled correctly, so that it is easily found later when it is needed.

- Trash it means that you touched it once and it is not needed again. If you can't handle the email, schedule the email, or print and file the email, it must be trash. Saving your friend's witty email is a waste of time. Don't worry, the same person will send you another one soon!

One other problem with the email's nonproductive time is how you are viewed by others while you are glued to your phone or computer. You can come off as unapproachable while you appear to be busy or uninterested in helping a client. Don't forget who is paying your bills. Too many salespeople waste the day away with distractions that lead to other distractions like social media and games on phones. If you even need to touch these things daily, do it when you are not stealing time from people who are important to you at work and at home.

Hopefully, using email as an example served you well in understanding the Touch It Once Principle. When you have scheduled productivity, you will enjoy an increase in the quality of your work and personal time.

Putting The Touch It Once
Principle to Work

The following questions are designed to gain a working understanding and real application in your business and in your life. Always try to answer the following questions before moving on to the next principle. This will provide you the opportunity to reflect on the value of each principle as a standalone concept. The more quality effort you apply to your answers, the better chance you will see immediate and lasting results from the value of each principle. The questions below are the same at the end of each chapter. Being cognizant of this will allow you to develop an action plan for putting the principles to work as you continue to read.

Define the key points of this principle that you will apply in your business.

Give an example of how the author demonstrated the principle.

Write three real examples of what you would say to your clients to show how you can apply this principle in your business.

Define three plans to exemplify ways that this principle will increase the quality of your selling process, margins, volume, and relationship with your clients.

Write an analogy of how this principle would apply outside of business.

FORTY-NINE

BE MANAGEABLE

This principle has a simple yet powerful message. When you help others first, you win. Allow your clients to manage you. They came in for your product so they already know that they want it. Try to keep this principle that simple. Listen to what your clients want and why they selected you and your product. Reinforce their good decision by letting them manage you through the selling process. And finally, let them buy. Try to stay out of their way by not confusing them with more information than they need.

Along with being manageable by our clients, we must be manageable by our supervisors. Your sales manager needs you and you need them. You have different jobs and if you don't do yours, the manager can't do theirs. It is your job to sell the product; it is your manager's job to help you make the deal better. If you don't sell the product and the manager has to do your job, theirs will be compromised. Let your manager help guide and structure your sale so you can concentrate on letting the client manage you toward their purchase.

One example would be when you go to your manager for help in closing the sale. If you allow your manager to give you a summary closing technique that will work in this situation, you are manageable. If you go out and use the technique, you are helping the clients see the value of what they came in to buy. Again, you are allowing your clients to manage you as they want help in making a decision on which product to own. Don't lose sight of the reason why your clients came to your business. They came to own one of your products.

We do not know what our clients or managers know. Listen to the buying and selling signals that are sent out and received by both. Allow yourself to be managed, but stay on course within your selling system. Your selling system is designed to help your clients as you ask the questions that they may not know to ask, the questions that just may be keeping the clients from giving a salesperson enough information to help them purchase.

When you are manageable, you let people you care about tell you what they need. Since they are with you, they need you and your product. Don't worry about your need for a sale. The client must purchase or they have wasted a day off that they will have to repeat if they want your product. Focus on the client managing you into letting them purchase your product. When the client wins, you automatically win too.

Putting The Be Manageable Principle to Work

The following questions are designed to gain a working understanding and real application in your business and in your life. Always try to answer the following questions before moving on to the next principle. This will provide you the opportunity to reflect on the value of each principle as a standalone concept. The more quality effort you apply to your answers, the better chance you will see immediate and lasting results from the value of each principle. The questions below are the same at the end of each chapter. Being cognizant of this will allow you to develop an action plan for putting the principles to work as you continue to read.

Define the key points of this principle that you will apply in your business.

Give an example of how the author demonstrated the principle.

Write three real examples of what you would say to your clients to show how you can apply this principle in your business.

Define three plans to exemplify ways that this principle will increase the quality of your selling process, margins, volume, and relationship with your clients.

Write an analogy of how this principle would apply outside of business.

FIFTY

GO PRO

By virtue of you working at your business, your client's perception is that you have the qualifications and training to provide professional service. This should be the case. Unfortunately, many salespeople elect to not Go Pro in their sales career. The best way to present this principle will be to define athletes at different levels of their development. As they are defined, ask yourself, Does this level of commitment describe where I am in my career growth?

First there is the high school athlete. They have a coach for only the season. If they chose to not play beyond high school they only play during the season. They may think about their sport all year, but only work during the season or certain tournaments. Seasonal and show salespeople work the same way. They cram the knowledge to sell into what they can learn right before the season or show starts. These salespeople do not build a client base or do much follow-up as they will not be there when the client comes back. Many appear to be great salespeople because they sell in bursts.

This occurs because there is no tomorrow for them, there is only today to make and close a sale. If you play at the high school level your product and sales knowledge is not at the level your client and employer should be expecting, but you know enough to make the team and get through the season. After all, you didn't or don't plan on making a career out of sales: it's just a job for now.

At the college level, coaches and training are available all year. While it is still not your job, it could be your passion or a way to get an education if you are on a scholarship. Unless you are one of the elite players, your chances of going pro are limited. So while you may love your sport, your education is your job. If you are a salesperson playing at the college level, you have trainers and sales managers available to you all year long. The question is, how much of the resources that are available to you do you use? Do you only go to the weight room during team practices? Do you only study game film when you are at a team meeting? At the college level of sales, you are not held accountable by your manager to study your products and presentations outside of work. That time, they know is for your study of your future career. If you are a salesperson playing at the college level, you have not yet made the commitment to sales as your career choice, and therefore do not do what it takes to go pro.

At the professional level, playing your sport is your job. You are expected to work out and maintain certain conditioning levels even in the off-season. You are expected to memorize playbooks that are hundreds of pages long and be ready to execute any play, at any time without notice. Since you are paid to play, your coaches, teammates, and fans expect a professional level of performance at all times. Your paycheck (along with knowing that there are many others who would love to take your position) should be your motivation. All of the above is true for professional salespeople. Professional salespeople know that there are few jobs that still pay what a person is worth. The harder you work, the more product you know and sales techniques that you master, the more you will make. Professional salespeople are always to work on time and do not have to be told to study or follow-up with clients. They are always prepared to execute the coach's plays to perfection. They hold up their share of the workload for their teammates. And one of the most important things that a sales professional always does is represent the business correctly in public.

While going pro is all your management needs, you may decide to ask yourself: Do I want to do what it takes to be a franchise player? Franchise players do everything that a professional does, but at a higher level beyond the coaches' expectations. When strength training practice is over, the franchise player will stay in the weight room longer to achieve more so they can outperform expectations. They will study game film all day and then take it home at night and study again. They don't just have a professional work ethic, they have a passion for their sport and for greatness. These passions are what separates them from the pack of professionals.

If you want to be a franchise salesperson, start by asking if you have the real passion for it. Passion in this case would be defined by the powerful or compelling emotion such as love or hate. You love the game, love to win, love the feeling of being a winner, love being appreciated for your efforts, hate losing, hate not being the best, hate letting your team, coaches and family down by not making the sale. All of these and more fuel the passion for franchise players to not just practice, but to practice at faster than game speed. They will all tell you that the real game unfolds in slow motion and is easy after what they did to prepare.

So, at what level do you want to be a sales professional? If you are playing at the high school or college level, you have not given the sales profession a real chance. Only after you train and gain the knowledge of a professional will you truly know if the effort you put in is worth the paycheck. Who knows, after you become a professional, you might get the passion to become a franchise player. If you are reading this book, you are already on your way!

Putting The Go Pro Principle to Work

The following questions are designed to gain a working understanding and real application in your business and in your life. Always try to answer the following questions before moving on to the next principle. This will provide you the opportunity to reflect on the value of each principle as a standalone concept. The more quality effort you apply to your answers, the better chance you will see immediate and lasting results from the value of each principle. The questions below are the same at the end of each chapter. Being cognizant of this will allow you to develop an action plan for putting the principles to work as you continue to read.

Define the key points of this principle that you will apply in your business.

Give an example of how the author demonstrated the principle.

Write three real examples of what you would say to your clients to show how you can apply this principle in your business.

Define three plans to exemplify ways that this principle will increase the quality of your selling process, margins, volume, and relationship with your clients.

Write an analogy of how this principle would apply outside of business.

FIFTY-ONE

TEAM PLAYER

There may be some early confusion when you look at the title of this principle and you think about salespeople who are paid on commission. The usual accepted definition of Team Player would be a selfless person who cares about the welfare of his teammates and winning above any personal needs. In sales, this won't pay the bills.

The Team Player needed in sales is similar to the Ryder Cup in professional golf, or Davis Cup in professional tennis. Both are teams stacked with the best available athletes to compete for their country. What makes these teams different than a football or basketball team is that they each must win their own match play. They may coach each other and cheer on their teammate, but at the end of the day they have to win their own individual match. What makes this a professional game is still the money. Playing on an international stage means big-time endorsements for the showmen and winners. Their national rankings are also affected by the quality of their play, which again translates to a paycheck.

Professional salespeople can train together and practice together, but when it comes time to present your product to your client, it is just you and your possible commission. Top salespeople understand the importance of their sales teammates winning. When the other salespeople do well, the inventory is better, the advertising budget is better, and the bonuses are better. When the entire team is doing well, everyone benefits from a profitable business.

As you grow with your team, you know that each of you has different strengths in sales. Some sell to different clients better, some have different product knowledge and some have not developed all of the skills in certain parts of their presentations. Knowing this makes turning your client to a teammate another possible way to win. If you give the client to a more skilled or knowledgeable salesperson, you can enjoy splitting a commission as opposed to getting the whole commission of a no sale.

The danger of being too much of a team player in sales is when you are called upon too often to help others at the cost of taking your own clients. It is easier to sell to your own client then to take a turn from another salesperson and fix their possible mess. Also, if you take over another salesperson's client, you may have to start over from the beginning in the selling process. This client may have been at your business for three hours and is hungry and tired. Now you have to treat them as if they are brand new and sell something completely different than what they are not liking and for possibly only half of the commission. Commission-wise, you may have been better off helping the next client than trying to fix someone else's problem.

Now if this doesn't sound like being much of a team player, look at your job description. If it doesn't say work for others for half and possibly no pay, your management doesn't want you to focus your energy in that direction. In fact, your management exists to help others grow and is there to help a struggling salesperson through the selling process. It is in their job description.

There is an old saying in sales: "Your job description is your pay plan." This simply means that if you are paid on commission, your job is to make a sale or you don't get paid. It is imperative to your success that you keep your focus on this throughout the day. You need to be with clients, training, studying, or doing follow-up at all times throughout the day. The analogy is the same for a service technician who is paid on a flat rate. Who are they billing their time to: a paying client, warranty, or the sales department? If they are walking around carrying a wrench with no billable client, there will be no paycheck.

This principle, Team Player, means that you support, study, train, and cheer on your sales teammates, but when you are called on to perform, it is just you and your client. Be sure to help others whenever you are not in a position for a sale yourself. Be sure to do all of your sales side work so the product is ready for you and your associates to present. But above all win your match, for it will also help your team!

Putting The Team Player Principle to Work

The following questions are designed to gain a working understanding and real application in your business and in your life. Always try to answer the following questions before moving on to the next principle. This will provide you the opportunity to reflect on the value of each principle as a standalone concept. The more quality effort you apply to your answers, the better chance you will see immediate and lasting results from the value of each principle. The questions below are the same at the end of each chapter. Being cognizant of this will allow you to develop an action plan for putting the principles to work as you continue to read.

Define the key points of this principle that you will apply in your business.

Give an example of how the author demonstrated the principle.

Write three real examples of what you would say to your clients to show how you can apply this principle in your business.

Define three plans to exemplify ways that this principle will increase the quality of your selling process, margins, volume, and relationship with your clients.

Write an analogy of how this principle would apply outside of business.

FIFTY-TWO

KNOWLEDGE TRUMPS FEAR

For knowledge to win out over fear, fear must be identified and disproven. A salesperson's fear can feel as real as if there was an impending danger. This fear can paralyze a salesperson's ability to remember what to say at the time it needs to be said. The fear comes from being on commission, being in a sales slump, being pressured to perform at a higher level, coming off a poor week or month, and generally not knowing where your next sale is coming from. While all of these fears seem real, they must be forgotten when you face your next client. The past is not relevant to your next client, only the present and their future counts.

Think of a skier who has stiffened up while riding the chairlift to the top a mountain. As the skier looks down at the steepest slope he has ever seen, fear takes over. When this happens, his already stiff body becomes even more rigid. Now he can't bend his knees and carve a turn to slow down properly. Because he scared himself to paralysis, he will most certainly fall. The well trained skiers get off the lift and stretch out.

They don't stand and look at the hill and freeze. They attack the hill with confidence and have a great experience.

Salespeople must do the same thing. If you have been sitting making follow-up calls for hours, when you stand up you will be stiff. You must take the time to stretch out mentally and physically. Then when you feel good, you are ready to help a client purchase. Your confidence will come from the knowledge you have acquired through studying your product and your sales process. The critical repetitions in role-playing have prepared you for anything that could be thrown in your direction. Your understanding of your selling process will allow you to be empathetic toward learning your client's needs so you can help them make a purchase.

In the movie *The Replacements,* the quarterback Shane Falco identifies his fear as quicksand: "You're playing and you think everything is going fine. Then one thing goes wrong. And then another. And another. You try to fight back, but the harder you fight, the deeper you sink. Until you can't move ... you can't breathe ... because you're in over your head. Like quicksand."[11]

This is a perfect example of a how a salesperson feels after going days without a sale. Like they are in over their head and that they are sinking. Salespeople, when faced with a selling slump, start changing everything in their selling process, even the parts that work. The more that they struggle to make a sale and skip selling steps, the quicker they sink. Excuses

[11] *The Replacements.* Dir. Howard Deutch. Perf. Keanu Reeves and Gene Hackman. Warner Bros., 2000. Film.

start to justify losing sales and a salesperson can even start to believe their new selling level is their new normal and acceptable.

The best way to stop sinking is to stop fighting the quicksand. Remain calm and go back to the fundamentals that you know are right. When you get back to using your selling system that has been proven to work, your knowledge will trump fear. Without fear, you can be loose and relaxed. When you are back to selling again, your confidence will return. The quicksand will dry up and you will gain traction to move forward.

Putting The Knowledge Trumps Fear Principle to Work

The following questions are designed to gain a working understanding and real application in your business and in your life. Always try to answer the following questions before moving on to the next principle. This will provide you the opportunity to reflect on the value of each principle as a standalone concept. The more quality effort you apply to your answers, the better chance you will see immediate and lasting results from the value of each principle. The questions below are the same at the end of each chapter. Being cognizant of this will allow you to develop an action plan for putting the principles to work as you continue to read.

Define the key points of this principle that you will apply in your business.

Give an example of how the author demonstrated the principle.

Write three real examples of what you would say to your clients to show how you can apply this principle in your business.

Define three plans to exemplify ways that this principle will increase the quality of your selling process, margins, volume, and relationship with your clients.

Write an analogy of how this principle would apply outside of business.

FIFTY-THREE

I Did My Job

The negative representation of the I Did My Job Principle is unfortunately observed too often in sales departments. It is when a sale is lost and a salesperson's justification is, "I did my job. It's not my fault that they didn't buy. I did everything my manager instructed." These lines are often followed by, "They weren't going to buy today. Our prices aren't good enough. We didn't have the right product. They can't buy until ..." All of these justifications from salespeople can almost make it seem that what they are saying is acceptable and true. One great line that came from a political debate went something like: Just because you say something over and over doesn't make it true. There is no justifying losing a sale. You just wasted the client's time and made no commission.

Think about the last time you watched a football game and it seemed that play after play, the running back ran straight into the pile at the line and was tackled for no gain, or a slight loss. As a fan, this would make you think that either the plays being called are horrible, or that the running back needs to stop running the same direction for it is clearly not working. If it is your team playing, you may even get frustrated or angry.

Now, watch the running back as he leaves the field after a third and out series. He goes by the coach, and the coach says, "Nice job, we'll get them next time." The coach smiles to keep his player loose and starts thinking about his defensive team that is now on the field. The coach in this case, is reinforcing the I Did My Job Principle. The running back can now go to the bench, after losing, and say that he ran the play that was called by the coach and it is not his fault that it didn't work. This doesn't turn out well for the coach's career.

And what about the running back? Once a new coach comes in, if the same running back can't find or create a hole to run through, their career is over. The new coach will not lose their job over a non-productive running back that cost the last coach his job. The new coach has no loyalty to this running back, and may have his own players he wants to bring onto the team.

In the story above, the coach is the sales manager and the running back is the salesperson. Great sales managers do not let their salespeople get away with passing blame for lost sales. They do not say that it is acceptable for a client to drive one or more hours to their business and not make a purchase. The manager knows that his salesperson didn't find or create a hole to run through. They simply ran to the line and fell down. The salesperson didn't look at the whole field of options. They just did what they thought the manager would find acceptable, and then just walked the client.

What's sad is that the salesperson is the first to lose after the client. The salesperson in this case may not see this. They just think that losing is part of the game and you have to take the bad with the good. This is just not correct. Great salespeople always find a way to make the sale. They live by the Kobayashi Maru Principle; to top producers, the no-win scenario doesn't exist. They find and create opportunities to make sales and never justify a loss. Losing just makes them mad. Then they get fired up. Then they run through objections like a bad arm tackle. Then they run to daylight. Then they score and win!

Top salespeople find it funny when they come to work after a day off and quickly make a sale when they know that nothing was sold the day before. They even make comments to the nonproductive salespeople that all the good customers only come in when they are on shift. For a while, the manager may enjoy the top salespeople making jabs at the bottom producers. Later, the manager will just find this to be frustrating that his bottom salespeople can't make deals.

The I Did My Job Principle does not allow for excuses or accepting the status quo in a sales department. Simply doing your job will not make you successful. You must do your job beyond your manager's and your own expectations. When you do, you will find yourself running in the open field. This is where great running backs, and great salespeople, have breakaway speed and demonstrate the true creativity in their craft. The challenge is that you need the power in your presentation to break through the line of defense before you can run to daylight.

This power comes from practicing your sales presentation over and over until you don't have to listen to what you are saying. When you don't have to listen to yourself, all of your focus can be on the playing field. You will see open holes that you didn't even know existed, yet were always there.

Putting The I Did My Job Principle to Work

The following questions are designed to gain a working understanding and real application in your business and in your life. Always try to answer the following questions before moving on to the next principle. This will provide you the opportunity to reflect on the value of each principle as a standalone concept. The more quality effort you apply to your answers, the better chance you will see immediate and lasting results from the value of each principle. The questions below are the same at the end of each chapter. Being cognizant of this will allow you to develop an action plan for putting the principles to work as you continue to read.

Define the key points of this principle that you will apply in your business.

Give an example of how the author demonstrated the principle.

Write three real examples of what you would say to your clients to show how you can apply this principle in your business.

Define three plans to exemplify ways that this principle will increase the quality of your selling process, margins, volume, and relationship with your clients.

Write an analogy of how this principle would apply outside of business.

278

FIFTY-FOUR

KNOW YOUR PRODUCT

A simple analogy for this principle would be dribbling a basketball. When you first start out, you look down and watch the ball as it hits the ground and comes back up. At what point, or what number of repetitions, do you feel the confidence to not look down and just dribble the ball? Some players, who never advance to playing the game well, don't master the skills to gain the confidence that the ball will come back if they don't look down. Now think of dribbling while running at different speeds, with different balls and on different surfaces. All of these variables could cause you to look down to find the ball.

The problem with looking down at the ball is that you can't watch the defensive player at the same time. While you are looking down, the defender is coming up to steal the ball and you don't even know this is happening. In the NBA there are teams that have huge home court winning percentages as their home court is distinctive. While this court may have an everyday feeling to the people who play on it daily, it may be an uncomfortable distraction to the competition.

Your product knowledge should be your greatest source of confidence. It is a variable in your sales presentation that you can learn and count on as a constant. The product in front of you is what you studied and what you know. The repetitions in presenting your product have allowed you to be prepared for any and all questions that your next client may ask. With superior product knowledge, you will find yourself looking your client in the eyes as you explain how a product works.

Your product knowledge is your home court advantage.

Your product knowledge will not just give you confidence, it will also give your client the confidence to make a purchasing decision today. This means that you have to know your product better than what is available on the internet. If your client believes that they will not learn anything more by shopping online, they can have the confidence to purchase.

It is also important to know your product's history and how your product is manufactured. Sharing that the manufacturer has been around since 1895 and how they evolved as a company to build this product will help your client feel like the factory warranty will support them after the sale. Your clients expect you to know why your company represents a product and how your company will stand behind it after the sale.

Knowing your product and being able present your product are two separate principles. The presentation part was covered by Principle Ten, Interactive Presentation. In that principle it is explained that you need to solve clients' problems with the features that are available on your product. In this principle, it is important to note that too much product knowledge can kill the sale.

The salesperson who feels the need to cover every nut and bolt may talk past the sale. While it is vital that your presentation is thorough and covers every feature, you must keep from going too deep for your client. Your clients want to know how to use the product and the applications for themselves. Most clients do not want to know the original equipment manufacturing of a wiring harness or at what temperature the metals were heated and cooled. Having this specific knowledge will give a salesperson confidence, but is not needed in a presentation to most clients.

The exception to the last paragraph would be the deliberate buyer. These are engineers and technical experts who love to know everything before making a purchase. While no one knows everything, you are at least expected to know more than the client who has been researching your product for five years before coming to see you. Don't worry, the knowledge they have is just from reading or listening to another client who has the same product. You have the product. Your knowledge is hands-on and real-life. You just have to teach these clients the applications of your product and they will purchase easily. Through their research, they already know that your product is the best or they wouldn't be with you. Show them why they are correct.

When you know your product, you can focus on your client and enjoy the company of someone who has a similar interest as yours: the product. When your client sees your genuine enthusiasm for the product it confirms that they have made the right choice. After all, if you are this excited to present something that you have presented hundreds if not thousands of times, this product must be something special.

Your client needs your knowledge, your enthusiasm, and of course an effective selling process to keep them moving toward owning the product. As you share your product knowledge, keep the presentation on task and all about your client. Be sure to not talk about how you would use the product. You are not the buyer spending your hard earned money on this product.

Last, be respectful of your client's time. When they ask to purchase, let them buy. Not everyone wants a full presentation. They may already know what they want and want to use it today. Get out of the client's way to your register. Never feel the need to say, "Wait, there are fifty more features you must see before you can buy." You are selling a good product. That's why your clients came to you. Don't talk past the sale. Too much information after a client wants to buy will take away their confidence and you will lose the sale.

Putting The Know Your Product Principle to Work

The following questions are designed to gain a working understanding and real application in your business and in your life. Always try to answer the following questions before moving on to the next principle. This will provide you the opportunity to reflect on the value of each principle as a standalone concept. The more quality effort you apply to your answers, the better chance you will see immediate and lasting results from the value of each principle. The questions below are the same at the end of each chapter. Being cognizant of this will allow you to develop an action plan for putting the principles to work as you continue to read.

Define the key points of this principle that you will apply in your business.

Give an example of how the author demonstrated the principle.

Write three real examples of what you would say to your clients to show how you can apply this principle in your business.

Define three plans to exemplify ways that this principle will increase the quality of your selling process, margins, volume, and relationship with your clients.

Write an analogy of how this principle would apply outside of business.

FIFTY-FIVE

CHESS

In the game of chess certain moves have been calculated to be statistically advantageous later in the game. For example, when both players are of equal skill the one who gets the opportunity to move first (the white pieces) will have a higher probability of winning. This occurs because the white pieces gain control of the board and stay on the offense for the entire game. When the black pieces (the person who makes the second move) are moved, it is for defense. The black pieces could go through an entire game without making an offensive move unless the white pieces make a mistake.

This is also true in sales. When a salesperson gets off to a good start in meet and greet, rapport is built. Then if the salesperson has the client agree with the selling process, and the salesperson carries it out ... the deal is done. The first move is critical as it sets up the relationship of everything that follows.

As in chess, if the person on offense makes even the slightest mistake, it could cost them the sale. For example, there are a list of questions that will take you off your game that you will not need to ask. Some of these questions are listed below.

- Do you generally buy new or used? What if the perfect product for the client is the one in your inventory that they didn't select? Now you can't even show the right product!

- What are your current monthly payments? Who cares? They are not buying the same product again in the same financial position. They could be wanting something that is possibly $20,000 more and they could owe $10,000 more on their trade than it is worth.

- How much do you think your trade is worth? Again, not relevant. If the client is making payments, they just want you to pay it off and get the new payments to fit within their budget. Why pick a fight over the value of a trade?

- Where else have you shopped? The client's response could be, "Great idea, we haven't shopped yet. We should see what else is out there." This will not end well for you.

- What's the best price you've seen so far? Then the client gives you a price that they saw on the internet that is much lower than yours. The price was not important because they didn't want to go five states away to make the purchase, but now it is.

- What other comparable models did you like? The client's answer is a model you don't carry. Why bring it up in the first place? If they liked the other model, they would have already purchased.

- When did you plan on making this purchase? This salesperson sounding question almost always makes the client feel pushed, and then they get defensive. To the salesperson the answer should always be, "We want to purchase right now." Since you already know the answer, why ask the question and change your offense to defense?

- How much time do you have today? The answer could be, "We only have fifteen minutes." Now you have lost the ability to take the time to deliver an A+ presentation. Again, why ask a question where the answer puts you in a position to play defense?

Great chess players think at least three moves in advance. This is why the game has so many different possibilities in the way it can be played and won. If you move a piece and consider all of the counter moves on the chess board, and then multiply the moves times the three next possible moves by your opponent; it is exponentially higher than most players are able to see during the time permitted in the game.

As in the game of chess, your selling process has taken into account most moves and countermoves in advance. One example would be early in the presentation when a salesperson says, "As I present this product to you I will source it from three areas: All available material in print to include brochures and trade publications; all available material you could find on the internet to include our website as well as the factory website; and finally, I will cover the material in the owner's manual that most clients don't get to see until they purchase." Now, after saying that you will cover all this material with the client, and you follow through in your product presentation, the client won't need to ask for a brochure at the end. Your chess move was made and it took into account what a client could say three hours later.

In chess, the term check means that the king is in jeopardy of being taken and the game being over. When a player is in check, they have to move out of check or block the move. One player usually takes control of the game toward the end and keeps their opponent in perpetual check while methodically picking off their remaining chess pieces. This takes away all chance of regaining an offensive position. The game quickly comes to an end when this occurs.

Great salespeople keep their clients in check throughout the selling process. They control what they say and what they ask. They keep the process moving so there is little time to go in a direction that will be nonproductive. They use all of the principles in this book to execute word tracks that have been practiced to perfection. There is no question asked or time scheduled in the selling process for the client to ask a question that will take them out of check. Your selling process should be methodically executed.

As in chess, great salespeople are ready for all counter moves because of the practice they put in before the actual game. Therefore they look like they are making a quick reflexive move when actually they were expecting the move and had the counter move ready. If you practice and play the game of sales enough, you will become ready for anything that is presented. To your client your selling process will be stress-free as there will never be a place for conflict.

Putting The Chess Principle to Work

The following questions are designed to gain a working understanding and real application in your business and in your life. Always try to answer the following questions before moving on to the next principle. This will provide you the opportunity to reflect on the value of each principle as a standalone concept. The more quality effort you apply to your answers, the better chance you will see immediate and lasting results from the value of each principle. The questions below are the same at the end of each chapter. Being cognizant of this will allow you to develop an action plan for putting the principles to work as you continue to read.

Define the key points of this principle that you will apply in your business.

Give an example of how the author demonstrated the principle.

Write three real examples of what you would say to your clients to show how you can apply this principle in your business.

Define three plans to exemplify ways that this principle will increase the quality of your selling process, margins, volume, and relationship with your clients.

Write an analogy of how this principle would apply outside of business.

FIFTY-SIX

POOL

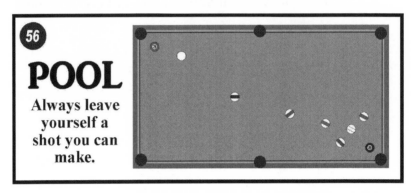

Have you ever watched a professional billiards match on television? The secret to winning is to always leave yourself an easy shot. After making a shot, the professionals skillfully put the right amount of English on the cue ball to leave it set up for making the next shot, and the one after that. In doing this, the other player never gets a turn to play. In sales, top salespeople are not only caroming one word track into another, but they are also leaving no others a turn to play.

Sometimes in pool, there appears to be an open or easy shot. If you are inexperienced, you walk up and take the shot. Then you look at the table only to notice that you left yourself no next shot that you can make. At this point, in pool, you would try to bury the cue ball and leave no shot for your opponent. Sometimes in sales, we have to do the same thing. If a client can't buy today, we want to make sure that our competition never gets the opportunity to make a shot with our client.

If we are leaving our competition no shot, it means that our client knows the differences between our product and services and those of the competition. Therefore the client has no desire or interest in shopping at another business. This can backfire if it is not done correctly. No client wants to hear you put down your competition, and in fact will get defensive for your competitor if they feel that you are speaking wrongly of them. The correct way is to talk about what features your product has that are different, and why they are important. It could be as simple as noticing that the client will need to go on the highway and your competitor doesn't sell highway products. Point out the differences in an educational way so that the client can come to their own conclusion that there is no need to visit the competition.

Great pool players see the whole table. They see shots that a novice would not see, or if they saw the shot, would never attempt to take it. Watching a double bank shot, a two ball shot, or even an English jump shot may be a "WOW" moment for a novice, but these are all well-practiced shots for professionals.

Professional salespeople see their entire game as well. They see all of the options on how and what to say and are always measuring the results. When they say what works to make a sale, it is because they have put in the time in practice to be prepared for what could come next. New salespeople think that professionals are naturals and make it look easy, but they don't see the time that was put in to play at the highest level. Top salespeople are always, as in pool, leaving themselves an easy shot.

Putting The Pool Principle to Work

The following questions are designed to gain a working understanding and real application in your business and in your life. Always try to answer the following questions before moving on to the next principle. This will provide you the opportunity to reflect on the value of each principle as a standalone concept. The more quality effort you apply to your answers, the better chance you will see immediate and lasting results from the value of each principle. The questions below are the same at the end of each chapter. Being cognizant of this will allow you to develop an action plan for putting the principles to work as you continue to read.

Define the key points of this principle that you will apply in your business.

Give an example of how the author demonstrated the principle.

Write three real examples of what you would say to your clients to show how you can apply this principle in your business.

Define three plans to exemplify ways that this principle will increase the quality of your selling process, margins, volume, and relationship with your clients.

Write an analogy of how this principle would apply outside of business.

FIFTY-SEVEN

WORDS MATTER

> # Words Matter
>
> ## We are judged by what we say.

This principle points out that our word selection has a great impact on how we are perceived. There are two thoughts on the use of large and impressive words when communicating with our clients. First, there are those salespeople who download apps that teach them one new word per day. They practice the word and search for places to insert the new impressive word into daily conversation. While some of these people just have a zest for learning, they may come off as pretentious. Then there are the people who just like learning a new word so that they can look and sound smarter. They don't just come off pretentious, they are pretentious. The intelligent clients look at them as if they are trying too hard to look smart, and the less knowledgeable clients feel that they are not to be trusted.

If you are selling a large-ticket product that has many technical aspects, your words must be industry-specific for a proper presentation. While the technical description could lose a novice to the industry, it may be necessary to use the correct terms in explaining how your product works. To help the beginners, you may need to slow down and answer questions and explain the industry-specific terminology along the way. These clients need a teacher, not a salesperson.

While using ostentatious words is important with the right client and in the right situation, the same words can turn off a client who has a hard time following what you are saying. The clients could feel like they will be viewed as uneducated if they stop you to ask what a word means. Some clients would rather not ask for help and leave than to be made to feel poorly and/or inferior.

With the exception of the technical products and clients, it is important to speak in TV English. Simply put, this means that the word you choose should be easily understood by all clients. The local news channels are judged by their number of viewers. To get more money from advertising clients, the news presenters need to keep their ratings high. The best way to do this is to not offend anyone watching their broadcast. Salespeople have the same challenges. To get repeat and referral business, your clients must like you enough to purchase as well as refer a friend.

What about the salespeople who use Good Ol' Boy English? Just as the technical salespeople use industry-specific terms, this relaxed form of English has its place as well. There are many truck, RV and boat salespeople who can pull it off as they are selling fun and leisure products. This relaxed

English can create a nonthreatening mood that they can carry throughout the selling process.

One other place you will find Good Ol' Boy English work effectively is in some rural areas. If everyone in a market area uses this relaxed English and you don't, you can come off as slick. In this case you are the outsider. If you don't use words that the client is comfortable with, you may actually be discriminated against.

While Good Ol' Boy English is effective with the right client and on the right product, it should not be a salesperson's default presentation style. Some clients have worked hard at their education and now don't enjoy being around people who are not at the same educational level. This is not to say that they are snobs. Rather, they just do not enjoy "liss'enen up to a lot of aints" in a sentence. As a salesperson, try to understand how your client wants to be served.

As noted earlier in this book, most major newspapers write at the sixth-grade level so that all readers can feel comfortable with what they are reading. If your clients don't understand your message then they will stop listening. As salespeople, we are faced with not being too intellectual or simple in our word choice. We must use the form of communication that our clients will find the easiest to comprehend and still not find offensive.

This is a difficult principle to apply because there are as many incorrect as there are correct ways to communicate with your client. As you work on this principle, remember you are perceived as what you say to your client, your manager, and the people you care about.

Putting The Words Matter
Principle to Work

The following questions are designed to gain a working understanding and real application in your business and in your life. Always try to answer the following questions before moving on to the next principle. This will provide you the opportunity to reflect on the value of each principle as a standalone concept. The more quality effort you apply to your answers, the better chance you will see immediate and lasting results from the value of each principle. The questions below are the same at the end of each chapter. Being cognizant of this will allow you to develop an action plan for putting the principles to work as you continue to read.

Define the key points of this principle that you will apply in your business.

Give an example of how the author demonstrated the principle.

Write three real examples of what you would say to your clients to show how you can apply this principle in your business.

Define three plans to exemplify ways that this principle will increase the quality of your selling process, margins, volume, and relationship with your clients.

Write an analogy of how this principle would apply outside of business.

FIFTY-EIGHT

WE DON'T KNOW

This is a simple principle. It means that we don't know what we don't know. After all, how could we? We wouldn't even know to ask the question to learn about what we don't even know exists. For salespeople, this gets in the way of not coming up with the right questions to ask a client. It also will keep a salesperson from giving the right answers that a client may need to make a purchase.

This principle gets a little sticky when a salesperson loses a sale and says, "My bad." To the manager who was working the deal with the salesperson, this seems like a diffusion of responsibility, almost as if the salesperson is minimizing the loss. All the manager hears is that the salesperson is not as committed to making the sale because as quickly as they take blame, they dismiss the ownership of the money lost.

The key to this principle lies in the idea that it is alright to take the heat off for not knowing what you don't know. It is not alright to take the responsibility away from losing the sale. Remember, when a salesperson loses a sale, the client and the business both lose. You, the salesperson, are totally responsible for helping the client make a purchase so that everyone can win.

After a lost sale, while the broken selling process is still in your mind, get help. Go to your manager and immediately ask what you need to learn or could have done. If there is still something possible to do, Do It Now. Your manager will appreciate that you care about not losing and that you want to learn from your loss.

Another point to this principle working is admitting that just because we don't know something doesn't mean that it doesn't exist. Sometimes salespeople lock on so tightly to what they are planning to say next that they don't keep their mind open to learn something new in the middle of their selling process. Every client is different. Your selling process, while it must have guidelines, must also be flexible enough to allow you to learn and create on the fly what your client needs. New salespeople struggle with this as they are trying to make a sale as well as earn their manager's respect.

When some salespeople are new to being paid on commission, they do not feel comfortable giving a presentation unless they have complete knowledge of their product and their selling process. While this is respectable and responsible, it is not very realistic. Your manager will outline your training process, and you must trust that your manager knows what you don't know. You are paid on commission and you need to get into the game. Make sure that whatever your manager asks you to learn, you study and learn it beyond their expectation and continually ask for more to learn.

While we never want to lose a sale, when you do lose a sale, see it as an opportunity to learn what you haven't been taught yet. If your manager has already taught you how to handle a situation, and you forgot, this is a problem. If your manager has to teach the same thing over and over to you, they will find a new salesperson that they only have to teach once. When your manager teaches you something, they expect that you know it and will apply it to your selling process. If you don't understand what your manager is teaching, ask questions while in training. It is easier for your manager to teach and you to learn in a classroom-type setting than in the middle of a sale with a client.

When you learn something new, write it down, practice it, and commit it to muscle memory. You don't want to try to remember what to say in the middle of working a deal. It is important that your manager sees you write and practice what they are teaching. So many managers talk about holding the same sales meeting every three months and watching their salespeople hear the information like it has never been said before. Don't be one of those salespeople.

We can't know everything, but we can learn and be ready for next time. Top salespeople put themselves out there in the thick of the game and trust what they know. When they come across something new, they get excited to learn another new thing that will make the sale now, and help with future sales opportunities.

Putting The We Don't Know
Principle to Work

The following questions are designed to gain a working understanding and real application in your business and in your life. Always try to answer the following questions before moving on to the next principle. This will provide you the opportunity to reflect on the value of each principle as a standalone concept. The more quality effort you apply to your answers, the better chance you will see immediate and lasting results from the value of each principle. The questions below are the same at the end of each chapter. Being cognizant of this will allow you to develop an action plan for putting the principles to work as you continue to read.

Define the key points of this principle that you will apply in your business.

Give an example of how the author demonstrated the principle.

Write three real examples of what you would say to your clients to show how you can apply this principle in your business.

Define three plans to exemplify ways that this principle will increase the quality of your selling process, margins, volume, and relationship with your clients.

Write an analogy of how this principle would apply outside of business.

FIFTY-NINE

CAPITALISTIC SOCIETY

Salespeople who get this principle understand that they are going to work for the money. They see selling as hunting for food. If you have no food in your house, you must go and get it or starve. In commission sales, it really is this simple. While it is not for everyone, all employees in a company are reliant upon the hunters and rainmakers. If no one makes a sale, all of the support and service staff who are not on commission would not have jobs. It is the risk takers, the hunters, who have the most to lose and all of the pressure to perform well with the next sales opportunity. They don't know when the next meal is coming so they have to make this one count.

While this might sound harsh to a non-salesperson, this is reality. Top salespeople do not go to work for social esteem, existential rewards, or even self-fulfillment. They go to work for the money and what they can do with it once it is obtained. With money they can feed their families, provide education, vacation, and buy what they want. Being on a salary or fixed income does not allow a salesperson to be paid what they are worth. They are willing to take the risk of being on commission for the possible rewards.

If your only source of food is killing the deer, you hunt. If you don't find a deer, you keep hunting. If you don't like the kill shot, become a farmer. If it doesn't rain and your crop doesn't grow, you starve just the same as the hunter. Hard work is what built this capitalistic society we live in today. Anything worth obtaining has work and risk associated with the prize. Salespeople have one target: to make the sale! It is not harsh. In all lines of work your project must be complete before you are paid. The difference is simply that the salespeople are the ones who are selling and presenting the project.

In this capitalistic society, we have been given the opportunity to build our client base as large as we can and want, based only on how hard we work. Top salespeople are easy to identify early in their careers. They are completely focused on the next sales opportunity. They don't let themselves get involved with anything that won't make them money. In regard to the gossiping of he said, she said, they don't care. Top salespeople stay clear of social gatherings in the workplace and company politics. If it doesn't pay, they have no interest. They are at work to provide for themselves and their family. If they want or need social esteem, they call a friend and set up a time to meet after work.

It is fun to watch these top salespeople be motivated by life's events. When they have a new child, they sell more. When they need a bigger house, they sell more. When they have a kid going to college, they sell more. When they have to pay for a wedding, they sell more. When they want a new toy, they sell more. They never ask for a raise or to be paid more for doing the same job. When they want a raise, they give themselves the raise by working more efficiently and selling more.

If you are not sure if you belong in sales you should ask yourself if you are ready to take full responsibility for the risks and rewards that come with being on commission. If you have to think about this, you should take a salary job and rely on the commission salespeople to provide you with your clients to service. Top salespeople are decisive and don't miss the opportunity to make a sale. If they are, they understand that the deer will run away and they will have to go home and tell their family that there will be no meat on the table. Salespeople cannot only handle this pressure, it makes them thrive.

Putting The Capitalistic Society Principle to Work

The following questions are designed to gain a working understanding and real application in your business and in your life. Always try to answer the following questions before moving on to the next principle. This will provide you the opportunity to reflect on the value of each principle as a standalone concept. The more quality effort you apply to your answers, the better chance you will see immediate and lasting results from the value of each principle. The questions below are the same at the end of each chapter. Being cognizant of this will allow you to develop an action plan for putting the principles to work as you continue to read.

Define the key points of this principle that you will apply in your business.

Give an example of how the author demonstrated the principle.

Write three real examples of what you would say to your clients to show how you can apply this principle in your business.

Define three plans to exemplify ways that this principle will increase the quality of your selling process, margins, volume, and relationship with your clients.

Write an analogy of how this principle would apply outside of business.

SIXTY

WHEN/HOW TO LOSE

This is a tough chapter to write because it admits that sometimes we must lose. While this goes against every principle in this book, it still must be addressed. First, let it be known that just because we know we must take a loss every now and then, we still at no point should ever believe that the client in front of us is not going to make a purchase today. This chapter is about when and how it is acceptable to lose when we must.

This chapter will make more sense if you relate it to why the Tap Out rule was invented for Mixed Martial Arts. When your opponent has you in a hold that could break your arm, your leg or even your neck, it is better to tap out than to continue and be out of the game forever. When a salesperson loses their confidence or spirit, it could be the end of their career. Before you were put into this compromising position, let's break down the steps that got you here.

Before you climbed into the sales ring, your initial training was completed. Your knowledge of your product and selling process was learned at the best level possible. You studied and role-played. You allowed yourself to be coached for the upcoming client and the current market and inventory conditions. You were well rested and had no life distractions. You stretched out and were relaxed yet focused.

First, ask yourself, "Was I really prepared fully to face a client today?" If the answer is yes, and you still lost, you did your best job possible! Second, did you put in the effort? The last paragraph identifies the effort in training and preparation. The question is, did you do everything during the selling process to give yourself a chance to win? Did you use all of your training material, all of comparable inventory, your manager and other coaches to help you stay in the sale? Did you metaphorically reach muscle fatigue and your last breath? Did you use turn techniques to give another salesperson a chance to come in and try something different? If the answer is yes, and you still lost, you did your best job possible!

If you know that you put your best effort into your training and in the match, be proud of what you accomplished, but not satisfied. To be a great salesperson, total satisfaction can only come from winning. You must keep winning as the only goal, not finishing the fight or completing the marathon. You only get paid a commission when you win!

In the cases where you lose, be thankful that you earned the chance to play with a superior opponent and were able to have learned something for the next selling opportunity. Be proud of your effort and start training even harder for your next client. Sometimes losing can be your best teacher; you can better identify your weaknesses and fix the problems in your presentation. But know that losing has a cost; don't learn all of your sales lessons with live clients.

The best way to know when to lose will be if your manager throws in the towel. This means that your manager ends the selling process with your client and tells you to let them leave. You, in the heat of the sale, can't be asked to judge all that your manager can see from outside the ring. When your manager says, "That's enough." It's time to move on. Still it must be noted that top salespeople have to be involuntary forced off a client because they do not believe in and can't accept the no-win scenario.

The easiest way to not have to deal with losing is to win all the time. When you have to lose, be sure that you gave your best effort possible, and then learn for the next client.

Putting The When/How to
Lose Principle to Work

The following questions are designed to gain a working understanding and real application in your business and in your life. Always try to answer the following questions before moving on to the next principle. This will provide you the opportunity to reflect on the value of each principle as a standalone concept. The more quality effort you apply to your answers, the better chance you will see immediate and lasting results from the value of each principle. The questions below are the same at the end of each chapter. Being cognizant of this will allow you to develop an action plan for putting the principles to work as you continue to read.

Define the key points of this principle that you will apply in your business.

Give an example of how the author demonstrated the principle.

Write three real examples of what you would say to your clients to show how you can apply this principle in your business.

Define three plans to exemplify ways that this principle will increase the quality of your selling process, margins, volume, and relationship with your clients.

Write an analogy of how this principle would apply outside of business.

SIXTY-ONE

WHY

**Adults need
to know why**

When we communicate with very young children, we tell them what we want, and what we receive is based on their understanding of the request. As these children become teenagers, you can request all you want, but you will only get what they feel like giving. As these teenagers become adults, they have learned the word "No" and have no fear in using the word. Adult clients will sometimes say no just because you are a salesperson and they believe your sole existence is to try to sell them a product they may or may not want. Thus, clients may be defensive because of previously uncomfortable situations and feel that they have to say no to protect themselves.

The Why Principle means that to be effective with our communications and requests of adults, we must explain why we ask questions. Adults live in the Why world. They need to know why they are doing something before they will start the project. Adults, when they understand why things are important, prioritize the task and schedule it into their life. Without understanding why, the adult will just hear your words and no action will be taken.

The questions that salespeople ask adult clients are designed to help provide service in the purchase. To be effective with these questions, salespeople must explain why they are asking the questions. When a client knows that the information gathered by the question directly benefits their level of service, the client quickly volunteers the information.

Salespeople are in the business of adult education and their clients are their students. When the client is educated correctly, you could hear them say, "We had planned on shopping at your competitors today, but now there is no need because we know that nothing else we see will be as nice." Clients who say things like this have been given full presentations and are educated to their level of satisfaction. They can now take action and buy your product.

In the principle Get Permission First, we focused on getting the client to instruct salespeople to move to the next step in the selling process. The Why Principle will help the client manage salespeople better as they understand the direction they are heading. Most importantly, they know why the direction benefits them directly.

Sales managers are also in the education business as their salespeople are their adult students. As sales managers ask a salesperson to deliver a message or ask a client a question, the quality of the message delivered to the client can vary drastically. When the salesperson knows why they are asking the question, the results will be more consistent. Managers, like salespeople, must take the time to explain why the information that they request not only benefits the client, but how it benefits the salesperson as well. Great managers have already figured out their profession is adult education.

This principle is not limited to your effective communication with your clients. If you start getting in the habit of explaining Why to your coworkers, managers, family and all the people in your life that you care about, the rewards could be endless. You will find that the quality of your communications will eliminate stress and increase the quality of performance. Clients will be more likely to refer business to you as they know the level of service that will be provided to their friends and family.

Why is the stimulant that makes things happen. As an adverb, Why simply asks what the meaning behind is or the cognitive thought is that motivates the behavior. As verbs are your action words, adverbs function as modifiers of the verbs. If you truly want your client to take action today, you must use your Why to modify, motivate, educate and direct the client through the selling process.

Putting The Why Principle to Work

The following questions are designed to gain a working understanding and real application in your business and in your life. Always try to answer the following questions before moving on to the next principle. This will provide you the opportunity to reflect on the value of each principle as a standalone concept. The more quality effort you apply to your answers, the better chance you will see immediate and lasting results from the value of each principle. The questions below are the same at the end of each chapter. Being cognizant of this will allow you to develop an action plan for putting the principles to work as you continue to read.

Define the key points of this principle that you will apply in your business.

Give an example of how the author demonstrated the principle.

Write three real examples of what you would say to your clients to show how you can apply this principle in your business.

Define three plans to exemplify ways that this principle will increase the quality of your selling process, margins, volume, and relationship with your clients.

Write an analogy of how this principle would apply outside of business.

SIXTY-TWO

TIME DOES NOT EQUAL EXPERIENCE

Many salespeople and sales managers are proud to tell you how many years they have in the business. You may want to believe that time equals experience and knowledge, but this is not always the case. Would you go to a dentist who has 40 years of experience without continuing education or without updating their technology and equipment? Experience is valuable, and time is the only teacher, but your clients today want the full package.

At Sobel University a class doesn't go by when you don't see both types of experienced salespeople. First, there is the student who has had enough success in sales over many years that they are confidently set in their ways. From where they sit, life makes sense. They are making as much as they need and are living within their budget. They are closing sales at an acceptable level compared to the others that they work with, so they see no need to change anything. With their self-confidence and pride, these students are identified early by the other students as the old-timers who are set in their ways.

The second type of student at Sobel University with years of experience is the salesperson who has gotten this far in life by keeping up with the times. They know that you have to adapt to survive and thrive in the ever-changing competitive marketplace. These salespeople are at class to make changes and have a chance for a pay raise. They know the reason they were sent to class: Their business wants to improve the level of their performance. The salesperson is happy that the business owner is spending money on their education.

This second type of salesperson is always heard saying, "I wish that I would have learned this twenty years ago!" They also tell the class that time on the job does not necessarily add up to knowledge, and that many experienced salespeople could have been doing the same thing wrong again and again over many years.

The new salespeople today do not have to unlearn any bad habits, and can start fresh with what works today. The new salespeople, while they have no experience of their own, make up for it by using others' experience.

If you are new to sales the only people that you want to listen to are the top producers or your sales manager. More often than not, the real top producers are not spending much time talking. They are busy selling. The people who do most of the talking are the bottom salespeople, as they have the time. The challenge is that in many businesses the top producer is not a real top salesperson, just the best one working at that business. Again, they are easily identified as they have time to talk about all of their sales experiences. If they have that much spare time, they are not really top salespeople.

> *If you have worked at the same job*
> *or in the same sales profession*
> *for thirty years, ask yourself:*
> *"Do I have thirty years on the job, or do I*
> *have one year on the job thirty times?"*

If you worked in a warehouse and did the same line selection work for thirty years, what new business skills would you expect to acquire? Time does not necessarily get you experience, it is just time.

Experience is defined by what we learn either through the course of living or an observed event. Experience then comes from how we take in and process the information and prepare it for use in a needed situation or action. While you can't buy experience at the store, you can learn from others' experiences. Just be sure that you qualify the person who is sharing their experience. Are they answering your questions, helping you with a specific sales challenge, or just sharing an old story to pass the time?

Top salespeople gain experience by listening to their clients as much as their coworkers and managers. Their clients

317

share why they purchase this specific product, how they use the product and helpful tips on applying the product to their personal needs. The key to this principle is to be open and ready to receive new experiences that will help you grow to the next level of sales. With experience, you will recognize similar situations that you have encountered before. When faced with the same challenges as before, you can use your experience to give you more options to make the sale.

Experiences are something we should be seeking to learn and grow. Without new experiences we cannot stay current with the ever-changing times. Relying on past and possibly outdated material will not serve salespeople well, as their clients are getting more and more knowledge quicker than ever. The world is changing fast and our best experiences are yet to come.

Putting The Time Does Not Equal Experience Principle to Work

The following questions are designed to gain a working understanding and real application in your business and in your life. Always try to answer the following questions before moving on to the next principle. This will provide you the opportunity to reflect on the value of each principle as a standalone concept. The more quality effort you apply to your answers, the better chance you will see immediate and lasting results from the value of each principle. The questions below are the same at the end of each chapter. Being cognizant of this will allow you to develop an action plan for putting the principles to work as you continue to read.

Define the key points of this principle that you will apply in your business.

Give an example of how the author demonstrated the principle.

Write three real examples of what you would say to your clients to show how you can apply this principle in your business.

Define three plans to exemplify ways that this principle will increase the quality of your selling process, margins, volume, and relationship with your clients.

Write an analogy of how this principle would apply outside of business.

SIXTY-THREE

ENABLERS

Enablers in a business are the average or below average salespeople who shower their top salesperson with accolades of greatness until they believe they are truly great. This empowerment or elevation of status, if not earned, can make a good salesperson average and allow the rest who perform even lower to justify their position. If the top salespeople in your industry sells twenty products per month, and your top salesperson only sells six, they are not a top salesperson. To celebrate these salespeople would be to let the salespeople just below them believe that they are doing a good job.

In this case, the salespeople who are really below average will start to believe that six is a good job. After all, if all they see is the top salespeople selling six products and receiving salesperson of the month awards and bonuses, what else could they believe?

Then a business owner goes to a conference and learns that top salespeople in their industry really sell twenty products per month. The business owner asks questions until he finds out what the other businesses or salespeople are doing to produce almost four times what he already thinks was a good job. If he finds a different selling system (or in many cases just having or implementing a selling system), first he has to go through his own paradigm shift. His entire belief structure has to change to be willing to do the work it takes to change behaviors. This is not easy when he has been praising poor performances because they are the best he has ever seen.

The hard part of the change will come when the business owner tries to implement changes in his business. The top salesperson has to come to grips that the job they are doing would make them below average anywhere else and that the salespeople below him would not even have jobs. Everyone in these businesses have enabled each other to believe that the job they were doing was acceptable. Now, their entire belief structure has been shaken to the core.

This principle's title, Enablers, means to give power or authorize behaviors and reinforce the actions as to make them credible or acceptable. Giving power to below average salespeople who have not truly earned the position will sometimes create many unwanted problems in business. This was witnessed when a salesperson named Fred (not his real name) became so impressed with himself for being the top in his business that no one liked working with him. He constantly told everyone how bad they were and how the management didn't know what they were doing. While he only sold eight products per month in an industry where the top salespeople averaged fifteen, he was the best he had ever seen. The other salespeople who sold four to five looked bad compared to him, and conversely, he looked great to the other salespeople and managers.

Then one day, the owner brought in a business consultant and trainer. At first, the trainer struggled because everything he said was contradicted or challenged by Fred. During a break, Fred even cornered the trainer outside and proceeded to yell and swear at him. Fred said that he was the best and that no one could be doing the numbers that the trainer was saying. Because the trainer was not new to his profession, he let Fred go off while the other salespeople watched through a window. When Fred was through yelling, the trainer calmly said, "Your business owner brought me in to teach new material that he doesn't know. There may be some material that will give you a pay raise." Fred sat through the rest of the course with his arms folded and made sure that everyone in the room knew that he didn't approve of the business decision to bring in an outside trainer. After all, he was the best and no one could know more than him.

One year later, the trainer ran into Fred at an industry convention. Fred had sought out the trainer to thank him for changing his life. Fred was now averaging twenty sales per month and enjoying the fruits of his labor. While the other salespeople in that business still believed that Fred was the best, they had moved their averages to more than ten sales per month. Fred stopped justifying his position and spent the time on improving his game.

Before the four-minute mile was broken, the sports and medical community had the athletes convinced that if anyone ran the mile in less than four minutes, they would surely die. Knowing this, the elite runners trained to get to four minutes. After all, who wanted to die? Then one day, the English track athlete Roger Bannister broke the four-minute mile. Once he accomplished this new record, more than one hundred different athletes from all over the world in the next month beat the four minute mile as well. It is amazing the power that Enablers have when it comes to lowering or raising our own expectations.

Many managers are guilty of enabling average salespeople as well. Maybe they simply do this because they don't want to deal with the headache of listening to the Fred in their business yell and swear. It could be that managers put up with average salespeople because they have no one better. Training is the only solution to making the necessary paradigm shift. Managers many times cannot get mad at low performers because they haven't given them the skills to perform.

In the sales industry, we can't ever believe that we have hit the top. If or when we believe this, we will only train to that level and miss the opportunity for greatness. Salespeople must be courageous explorers. Never knowing what will come next, but trying to be prepared and open for all options.

Putting The Enablers Principle to Work

The following questions are designed to gain a working understanding and real application in your business and in your life. Always try to answer the following questions before moving on to the next principle. This will provide you the opportunity to reflect on the value of each principle as a standalone concept. The more quality effort you apply to your answers, the better chance you will see immediate and lasting results from the value of each principle. The questions below are the same at the end of each chapter. Being cognizant of this will allow you to develop an action plan for putting the principles to work as you continue to read.

Define the key points of this principle that you will apply in your business.

Give an example of how the author demonstrated the principle.

Write three real examples of what you would say to your clients to show how you can apply this principle in your business.

Define three plans to exemplify ways that this principle will increase the quality of your selling process, margins, volume, and relationship with your clients.

Write an analogy of how this principle would apply outside of business.

SIXTY-FOUR

CHECKERS

Checkers, draughts or even the ancient game from Ur of Mesopotamia dating from 3000 BCE, while it has been referred to as many things over the centuries, checkers has maintained its integrity as a game. The basic rules are the same, the board is the same, pieces are the same and the game still is only played by two people. There are very few, if any, games that are played today that were played more than 5,000 years ago. To weather the test of time, the game has to have provided enjoyment, challenge and be able to be played at many age levels. The rules had to be simple and easily passed down from generation to generation.

Picture a father and son sitting down to enjoy a game of checkers. The son has a jump opportunity and elects to take another move. The father on his next move takes the piece that didn't make the jump and moves his own piece. The son, not knowing the rule that if you have a jump you must take it or lose your piece, is now angry. What set out to be a relaxing, enjoyable evening has been lost to accusations of cheating and not playing by the rules. Both the father and son may never play the game of checkers again and it will be lost to future generations.

This is the same situation that occurs when clients come to play with salespeople. The clients are excited for the prospect of purchasing and using their new product. The salesperson is excited about helping a client satisfy their purchasing needs and getting a commission. The challenge begins when all of the rules to the game are not laid out and agreed upon before they start playing.

When the client is expecting to look at products to decide what they want, and the salesperson wants to not waste the client's time looking at the wrong product, their rules to the game may be different. This difference may lead to the client feeling that the salesperson is not giving them good service or doing what they want. The salesperson knows that certain products will definitely not work for the client and out of respect for the client's time doesn't want to show a product that will not do the job needed. Because the client and the salesperson care, this leads to stress for both parties.

The principle, Checkers, is a kids' game that is easy to play, low in cost and has simple rules. To stand the test of time there had to be little stress and much enjoyment. For the players to wish to play many games with the same opponent the winners and losers must have both really won. They enjoyed the time together and would do it again.

Your sales presentation and process must be the same. All the rules must be defined and agreed upon before you start. The rules must be like a kids' game. They must be simple, easily understood, fair for both the client and the business, allow for fun, and above all, provide no stress.

When a client and a salesperson are playing by the same rules there are no surprise moves. The salesperson learns of a client's wants, needs and budget. The salesperson proceeds to only show products that will work for the client. The salesperson will never be over budget at the end of a presentation or trying to employ a new set of rules.

When a client enjoys the game (sales presentation) they make a purchase. They are excited to use their new product and refer others to the salesperson. The salesperson also enjoyed the time they spent with the client and has been heard saying, "Those were really nice people!" When the client has questions after the sale, the salesperson remembers them as being nice and can't wait to give them continued service.

Is checkers just a kids' game? This game taught us competition and enjoyment of games, fair play, rules, how to win, and how to pick ourselves back up from defeat. The game taught us how to enjoy and respect the other's company, even if we were fierce opponents. Salespeople are still playing Checkers daily with their clients and enjoying all of the benefits of the game.

Putting The Checkers Principle to Work

The following questions are designed to gain a working understanding and real application in your business and in your life. Always try to answer the following questions before moving on to the next principle. This will provide you the opportunity to reflect on the value of each principle as a standalone concept. The more quality effort you apply to your answers, the better chance you will see immediate and lasting results from the value of each principle. The questions below are the same at the end of each chapter. Being cognizant of this will allow you to develop an action plan for putting the principles to work as you continue to read.

Define the key points of this principle that you will apply in your business.

Give an example of how the author demonstrated the principle.

Write three real examples of what you would say to your clients to show how you can apply this principle in your business.

Define three plans to exemplify ways that this principle will increase the quality of your selling process, margins, volume, and relationship with your clients.

Write an analogy of how this principle would apply outside of business.

SIXTY-FIVE

NO ONE WALKS

Too often salespeople build relationships with their clients that get in the way of providing good service. While building a relationship with our clients is strongly encouraged, when it comes time for the client to leave, this could be a problem. The client says, "We need to leave to think it over" and the salesperson's response could be a quick, "Thank you for coming in today. Goodbye." (This thought should not leave you believing that you shouldn't build a great relationship with your client, but rather don't let a simple comment they make get in the way of helping them purchase today.) The salesperson erroneously believed that the client saw all that was available and needed time to think about their decision to purchase. The salesperson may not see all of the options available or have forgotten that the client already decided to purchase before they came to your business.

Many salespeople lack the confidence to ask for the order, or even to keep the client at their business until the client has been given every chance to purchase. Some salespeople do not want to be pushy or apply pressure to their client. These salespeople are looking at this all wrong. They are thinking about what they have experienced in the past, rather than what their client is experiencing now.

If you are following the correct selling system and the principles in this book then you know that every time you open your mouth, it is for the client. If you don't help the client, someone else will. When you know that you are the best person to purchase from, you will not need the confidence to apply pressure to make a sale. Your client will buy from you because they can clearly see that you are the best.

This principle comes from the phrase, "No one walks until the manager talks!" Salespeople are viewing their presentation at ground level. They see what the client sees and hear what the client hears. Your manager however, has a view from twenty thousand feet. When the salesperson has said all they can think of to help a client purchase, they should not be done. They should consult with a manager to see what other options are available to help the client go home today with a new product.

The manager can offer
additional knowledge
about the product that is being shown
and other options that the salesperson
might not know about.

*SOME OTHER FACTORS THAT THE MANAGER CAN
CONSIDER USING TO RE-ENGAGE THE CLIENT ARE:*

- The manager must consider the cost of bringing a client to your business.

- The manager must take the age of the inventory into account.

- Are there curtailments due on the product being shown or another product?

- Is the product discontinued?

- The skill level of the salesperson on that product.

- Where the client is coming from.

- Cost of the inventory.

- Is there a trade-in?

- The structure of financing available.

- If the product is new or preowned.

- Client's use (towing, hauling, storage, parking and daily use.)

- Availability of replacement for inventory.

- Delivery date needed.

- Salesperson's financial goals.

- In-stock or factory order.

- The competitions' inventories.

- Factory programs.

- Reconditioning costs of sale product and trade-in.

- Urgency of the client, the salesperson, and the business owner.

- Stability of the manufacturer.

- Client's ability to pay.

- Are all of the buyers present?

- Manager's confidence in the salesperson providing all of the particulars needed and accuracy of that information.

With many more options to consider, the manager must be given a chance to provide the client an opportunity to re-engage before they leave. This doesn't necessarily mean that the manager goes out and directly speaks with the client, although this is also a possibility. Most often, the manager will just give the salesperson additional things to try out before the client leaves. The principle, No One Walks, simply means that the manager must be given an opportunity to offer more options that could provide the client a chance to purchase today.

Business owners are very passionate about this principle because of the cost of bringing in the client. When the salesperson is heard saying that the client is theirs, the owners will object passionately. The owners paid to bring in the client, for the inventory, the building expenses, taxes and the salesperson's payroll. To the business owners, all of the clients that come in are theirs, not the salesperson's.

When a salesperson walks a client without checking with a manager, it is implied that the client can't buy today, or that the salesperson believes they will come back to them. Since so few actually come back, it very well could be that the reason they left in the first place is because they didn't like or trust the salesperson. The clients may have even lied and can't save face and purchase. This is an additional reason that salespeople must check with their manager before the clients leave.

The manager must be involved before the client leaves to take full advantage of the manager's experience and knowledge. The manager may have just helped another salesperson with the same challenges. The manager knows what other salespeople are available with the right skills to close this deal. And finally, the manager is motivated. Since the manager is also paid on commission, part of the sale belongs to the manager. When a salesperson walks a client, they are stealing from themselves, the manager, the business owner, and most of all they are stealing the right from the client to purchase from that business today.

Putting The No One Walks Principle to Work

The following questions are designed to gain a working understanding and real application in your business and in your life. Always try to answer the following questions before moving on to the next principle. This will provide you the opportunity to reflect on the value of each principle as a standalone concept. The more quality effort you apply to your answers, the better chance you will see immediate and lasting results from the value of each principle. The questions below are the same at the end of each chapter. Being cognizant of this will allow you to develop an action plan for putting the principles to work as you continue to read.

Define the key points of this principle that you will apply in your business.

Give an example of how the author demonstrated the principle.

Write three real examples of what you would say to your clients to show how you can apply this principle in your business.

Define three plans to exemplify ways that this principle will increase the quality of your selling process, margins, volume, and relationship with your clients.

Write an analogy of how this principle would apply outside of business.

SIXTY-SIX

BE READY

Professional athletes in football, hockey and basketball come out of the game for periods of time. When they go back into the game, they are expected to instantly perform at full game speed. A number of years back, there was an unpredicted power outage during the Super Bowl. While the power was out the players had to stay loose and ready to resume play at a moment's notice. One player was interviewed and was asked how he and his team were dealing with the indefinite delay. He responded by saying that he and his teammates are all professionals; they survive timeouts, turnovers and halftime breaks. He continued by saying that he and his team will be ready when play resumes.

Professional salespeople, like athletes, must be ready at any time to help a client. Picture yourself sitting at your desk making follow-up calls for two hours. When you get up to help a client who just came into your business you could be a little stiff from sitting so long. As your body moans at you, your clients notice that you are not moving so fast. This may not be the best start to your presentation.

When your clients got out of their car, they are excited. Their heart is beating fast. They are thinking about how great it will be to get their new product, and at the same time, they are thinking that they have to guard themselves from a salesperson who may try to take advantage of their desire for the new product. If you are stiff from sitting, it could be that by the time you get to the energy level the client needs, you could be perceived in a way that will deter from the selling process.

One way to stay ready is to mentally stretch out and stay loose. This means that if it is your turn to help the next client, read product information, study inventory, or literally stretch out. If your product presentation requires you to physically go and show the product, you have to be ready.

One of the worst ways to get ready would be to stand at the front of your business and talk to other salespeople. They could easily intentionally or unintentionally take you out of the game. If they feel the need to tell you about their last worst deal, how the lenders are not helping finance the products, how the manager is costing us sales, how the current inventory is inadequate and the weather is horrible for sales, you could be led off track. Listening to any negative conversation will not serve you well when you are getting ready to perform at game speed.

A great way to prepare to help clients would be to acknowledge your love of the game. When you see a client not being helped, you get excited because you love to help clients purchase as much as you love selling your product. Top salespeople can't wait to get in front of a client. They don't see it as a job. It is a game that they get to play as a career. Frequently you will hear top salespeople say, "Where else can you go to work to help nice people get what they want and at the same time get paid for doing what you love to do?!"

Many salespeople are called upon to take a turn in the sales process. This refers to another salesperson coming into your sale with no preparation time and taking over the sale from wherever you are in the process. The new salesperson knows that there is a problem or they would not have been sent in to the middle of another person's selling process. This salesperson not only has to repair the selling process, but also get the client recharged about going forward. This often requires the new salesperson to completely start over from the beginning as they are not heading in the right direction. These salespeople know that if the client left your business, they would be starting over at the next business, so why not here? With a cool head, they help the client as if they were a new or fresh sales opportunity.

When you love your profession, being ready is not a challenge. If you played basketball every Tuesday and Thursday evening in a league, you looked forward to going to play. You signed up to play, practiced, ate right, and got the right amount of sleep to play at your best level. A career in sales is the same. You selected your career and now you should want to perform at your best level.

What top salespeople do to get ready you may not see at work. They study in the evenings online, they come in early, they go the extra mile for their clients, they are ready to help other salespeople and managers, they eat right so that they are not slowed down during selling times, they get enough sleep to be able to work any hours needed at peak levels, and they love the practice in role-playing as much as the game.

If being a salesperson sounds more like a game than work, it is because to a top salesperson, it is a game. When you are ready to get into the game, your energy level spikes and your natural adrenaline kicks in. Your awareness goes up and you feel great! Being in the game means that you let the game consume all of your focus and attention so you are not living for the moment, you are living for the instant! When you are ready, you will enjoy sales at the highest level and gain incredible satisfaction in your profession!

Putting The Be Ready
Principle to Work

The following questions are designed to gain a working understanding and real application in your business and in your life. Always try to answer the following questions before moving on to the next principle. This will provide you the opportunity to reflect on the value of each principle as a standalone concept. The more quality effort you apply to your answers, the better chance you will see immediate and lasting results from the value of each principle. The questions below are the same at the end of each chapter. Being cognizant of this will allow you to develop an action plan for putting the principles to work as you continue to read.

Define the key points of this principle that you will apply in your business.

Give an example of how the author demonstrated the principle.

Write three real examples of what you would say to your clients to show how you can apply this principle in your business.

Define three plans to exemplify ways that this principle will increase the quality of your selling process, margins, volume, and relationship with your clients.

Write an analogy of how this principle would apply outside of business.

SIXTY-SEVEN

GO TO WORK TO WORK

WORK ETHIC

Picture a salesperson who knows that their sales opportunities usually do not come to their business until after 10:00 each morning. Could you picture the day starting with them coming in at 9:00 and then eating breakfast, reading the newspaper and socializing with the other salespeople about the game they saw last night? Then they may take a break and run to the local coffee shop. When they return, they finally sit down at their desk and call their friend to plan an event for this weekend. Now it is almost time for lunch. They arrange to meet their significant other at a local restaurant. Now it is 2:00 and they have missed the opportunity to call any clients back before the clients got busy themselves. Maybe they help a new client before they start making plans to go home and begin the evening's activities.

While this day may seem totally nonproductive, they did have lunch with their significant other and make plans for the weekend. This would be a rough day if the salesperson was paid on commission. If the salesperson puts too many days like this in a row, they will starve or lose their job.

Work ethic, as a principle, can be defined and recognized when what you believe has enough value to motivate you to perform at a strenuous enough level to result in physical and spiritual growth. Because of this definition, many people say that you get your work ethic from the example that was set for you by your parents or role models. If you were not exposed to a strong work ethic growing up, it is hard to picture what hard work really looks like.

When working out in a gym, will you ever push yourself as hard as a personal trainer would push you? In the absence of a good role model growing up, we need a personal trainer, manager, mentor, time management system, and a selling system. The systems will help salespeople stay on track and leaders will inspect, analyze, and push salespeople beyond where they would push themselves.

Top salespeople go to work to work. They start their day early and get their life in order before they come to work. When they show up, they are ready to start right away. Most top salespeople clean their desk each night and organize the work for the next day before they go home. They have projects scheduled for exact times, follow-up scheduled for an exact time, and time set aside for new clients. They move from one task to another with seamless efficiency. Most top salespeople bring their lunch to work and eat when they can. They understand that their client may dictate their schedule.

Top salespeople try to work seven hours in an eight-hour shift. They schedule two fifteen minute breaks so that they know when the break starts and ends. They schedule a thirty minute lunch. These salespeople know that if they work through a break or lunch, they did it for the commission. They never try to make up breaks or leave early.

Top salespeople know that they get all of the benefits of owning their own business without the liability. They don't have to pay for their inventory, advertising, building. and support staff. They understand that as a business owner they don't get paid unless they sell something. Being on commission there is no extra pay for longevity, just productivity!

Most salespeople with a strong work ethic will tell you that this is the first job they have ever had where they get paid what they are really worth. In non-commission state or federal government jobs, you get paid the same rate as the person with the same title with the same number of years on the job. While one of the two may really care and work harder, the pay is still the same. Salespeople can set their own pay based solely on how hard they want to work.

If you are lucky, you had a parent or teacher when you were very young who assigned you an almost unattainable task. You found the will to get it done. The mentor assessed and instructed you to correct your work. You finally finished the task, with pride in what you had accomplished. This set your work ethic for the future. Do it. Finish it. Do it correctly. Take a moment to celebrate the significance of your accomplishments. Then take on the next task with equal passion knowing that your hard work will lead to your future rewards and personal esteem.

Putting The Go to Work to Work Principle to Work

The following questions are designed to gain a working understanding and real application in your business and in your life. Always try to answer the following questions before moving on to the next principle. This will provide you the opportunity to reflect on the value of each principle as a standalone concept. The more quality effort you apply to your answers, the better chance you will see immediate and lasting results from the value of each principle. The questions below are the same at the end of each chapter. Being cognizant of this will allow you to develop an action plan for putting the principles to work as you continue to read.

Define the key points of this principle that you will apply in your business.

Give an example of how the author demonstrated the principle.

Write three real examples of what you would say to your clients to show how you can apply this principle in your business.

Define three plans to exemplify ways that this principle will increase the quality of your selling process, margins, volume, and relationship with your clients.

Write an analogy of how this principle would apply outside of business.

SIXTY- EIGHT

G-RATED

G-Rated in the motion picture industry means it's deemed suitable for viewers of all ages, or a "General Audience."[12] What happened to PG, R and X ratings? It seems what was R-Rated ten years ago has become PG today. What was X is now the new R. In adult magazines of the 1960's, they showed less skin than in many women's underwear television ads today. This is to say that underwear models today could have been centerfold features of the past. Has what we find to be acceptable today been deteriorated by time and desensitized our values?

As professional salespeople this is not an option. G-Rated is still G-Rated. The meaning of suitable for viewers of all ages must be a salesperson's credo. This book titled *Principle Centered Selling* is all about what it means to do things based on a set of values that are G-Rated. We are judged by what we do and what we say to our clients.

---

12   *Film Ratings.* Motion Picture Association of America, n.d. Web. 09 Sept. 2014. <http://www.mpaa.org/film-ratings/>.

In many selling environments the language has deteriorated to a point that even the workers would not want their ten-year-old to hear what was being said. A good test to evaluate your presentation (or the presentations being given around you that your client can hear) would be to ask yourself if you would leave your young kids in a room alone to hear the same message.

Many times salespeople and managers are just joking around and a client in earshot hears the wrong thing at the wrong time. If you know that you would not want your client to hear what you are saying you should never say it! This also applies to what your manager and other salespeople say that your clients can hear.

If you embrace the G-Rated Principle, you will go through the day like you are living in a Disney movie. High energy and creativity could motivate and inspire your direction. Everyone will go through the day smiling, knowing that the movies always end happily ever after. Your fun-loving attitude will be contagious to your clients and they will pass it on to your referrals.

G-Rated simply means that 100% of your clients will never be offended by what you say or do in their presence. You will find that what you do behind their back will often be reflected in your actions in front of your client. To be G-Rated means G-Rated all the time. No gray area, no question of intent, no excuses, just G-Rated; suitable for the viewing of all clients!

Putting The G-Rated Principle to Work

The following questions are designed to gain a working understanding and real application in your business and in your life. Always try to answer the following questions before moving on to the next principle. This will provide you the opportunity to reflect on the value of each principle as a standalone concept. The more quality effort you apply to your answers, the better chance you will see immediate and lasting results from the value of each principle. The questions below are the same at the end of each chapter. Being cognizant of this will allow you to develop an action plan for putting the principles to work as you continue to read.

Define the key points of this principle that you will apply in your business.

Give an example of how the author demonstrated the principle.

Write three real examples of what you would say to your clients to show how you can apply this principle in your business.

Define three plans to exemplify ways that this principle will increase the quality of your selling process, margins, volume, and relationship with your clients.

Write an analogy of how this principle would apply outside of business.

CONCLUSION

The challenge in writing this book came from the knowledge that learning and training is a moving target. In the time it has taken to write this book, and for you to read and apply its lessons, more new material has been revealed, studied and executed. As this book is about principles, the timelessness of the material will remain relevant while the examples may change to illustrate the concepts. As Principle Centered Selling is a first edition, more principles will be introduced as they become proven.

REMEMBER, TO BE A PRINCIPLE IT MUST MEET THE EXACT FOLLOWING CRITERIA:

1. All principles must be a catalyst to make sales.

2. Each principle is required to be able to stand alone on its own merits.

3. Each principle cannot violate another principle.

4. A principle can complement another principle, but still must be able to stand alone.

The principle Passion For Learning has been the stimulant for writing and sharing the contents of this book. As with all concepts that you will want to master, critical repetition and reinforcement will be the key to putting the principles to work. The chapters are purposely small so that they can be reviewed easily and frequently referenced in your selling environment.

Now that you have finished the book try to prioritize the principles for your life and business. If you review one a day, you will have more than two months of material. After reviewing the principles in individual study and sales meetings, sharing the concepts with others and putting them into your own selling process, you will find yourself using the principles several times a day and everywhere you go. You will notice when others use the principles with purpose, and sometimes by accident.

With the principles in this book mastered, you will enjoy a healthy relationship with your clients, coworkers, and managers and not have the need to take the pressures of your work home. As your affluence grows as a result of more sales, your original fear of being on commission will turn into your best asset. Realizing that salespeople get paid what they are worth is why you enter a field that has no financial limits. The more you learn, the more skills you master, the more you make. It's that simple.

It is my hope that you take the material in this book and build a first-class selling culture for yourself and your business. When you do, your clients will be thankful for having the opportunity to have received the best presentation of their life. As referenced many times in this book, only the best presentations will give today's educated consumers the confidence to stop shopping and make a purchasing decision now.

Good Selling.

ABOUT THE AUTHOR

Randy Sobel, President of Sobel and Associates, Inc., dba Sobel University, has made a career out of mastering the arts and sciences of selling as a profession for more than a 30-year period. Educated in industrial psychology with successful careers in manufacturing, distribution, insurance, professional sales training all with fortune 500 companies. Then followed that up with retail automobile, RV, power sport, marine sales and management. When earlier in this book it is referenced that many children had no inclination of wanting to be a salesperson when they grew up, Randy Sobel was playing salesperson games knowing exactly what he wanted for his life career.

Buying, selling and trading Matchbox and Hot Wheels cars from an early age was the first indication that Sobel had an aptitude for and extreme interest in sales. While most kids were playing with their toys, Sobel was figuring out his next marketing strategy. By eight years old, he had taken on a line of pens and pencils to sell at school. He purchased each of his products for five cents and retailed them for twenty-five to fifty cents. He then added locker pictures to his sales portfolio.

Wanting to get into the workforce early, Sobel applied for a minor work permit and broke a picket line to get on with a major grocery chain. Seeing this as his only way into the company, he crossed the line and earned a job when the strike was over. Working with that company part time while holding a restaurant job on the side, Sobel made his way through Junior and High School.

Continuing his work with the grocery chain through college, he moved to its distribution center, where he was allowed to conduct studies on how different stimulus increased productivity in warehouse workers. To Sobel, working hard was just an opportunity to expand his knowledge of how businesses work all while studying the workers and clients.

Since Sobel has made a hobby or game out of every working opportunity that is presented, he will tell you that he never views working as work, and always loves the game. On most Saturdays, you will find him at his dealership quietly taking clients through the entire selling process. With his annual closing ratio at close to 100%, he is more at home selling than in an office or on a golf course. As selling is his passion, this book is his view of how sales professionals should be presenting, how businesses and products should be presented, and how clients should be educated.

To Sobel, everything is calculated and measured in the selling process. The knowledge that he made available in this book is well proven by tens of thousands of students that have attended Sobel University over the past twenty four-plus years. But most exciting is what is to come. As Sobel still works the sales floor, his training has stayed current and relevant. His training clients as a result enjoy the new material as it increases productivity in their business year after year.

As much as he loves to sell and close, fortunately, he also loves to share his selling skills with others. Randy Sobel hopes you truly enjoy this book and it helps you in achieving your personal and financial goals.

ACKNOWLEDGEMENTS

To my loving wife, Lisa, for providing the support and drive, and not allowing for any compromises in the pursuit of excellence while putting up with the crazy extra hours needed to put this book together. You have been my strength and given me the energy to finish.

To Shauna Krell, for being able to think deeply on the selling process and be the muse for many principles.

To Jessica Sobel, for your editing skills and critical thinking.

To Jered Sobel, for questioning everything, holding me accountable, and caring enough to deliver the best.

To Stephanie Sobel, for being the motivation for many stories in this book.

To Nathan and Micky Sobel, for giving me the opportunity to become anyone I chose to be and the work ethic to follow through.

To Ellie, Doug, Mara and Gerald, for being understanding about the hours away from family needed to build a business and write this book.

To Marv and Sally Behar, for your positive support in all that I have worked on and completed.

To Howard Behar, for the grab onto a rising star concept and giving me a target.

To George Smith, for your character that allows principles to be grounded upon recognizing and doing the right thing.

To Melissa Prior, for holding me to deadlines, setting up the next challenge and following through.

To all of my coworkers over the many years, too many to list, who have motivated me and provided opportunities to be exposed to new principles.

To all of my valued clients, for implementing the numerous training techniques over many years that were necessary to prove these principles and for believing in these principles and making them part of your culture.

To Herb Kotkins, "There always alternatives."

To Herman Bass, for helping me to be a professional businessman and teacher.

To Bob Sheppard, for showing me the value of closing a sale.

To Curt Lance, Bruce Levin, John Nerney, and Paul Titus, for giving me leadership opportunities and trusting me to try my business concepts with your teams.

To all of my friends outside of business, thank you for humoring my creativity and allowing me to test my concepts with your valuable time and challenging me to always move forward with the unlimited support.

To the many thousands of top sales professionals who have put my training concepts and principles to work and proven their value I say, Thank You.

Principle Centered Selling

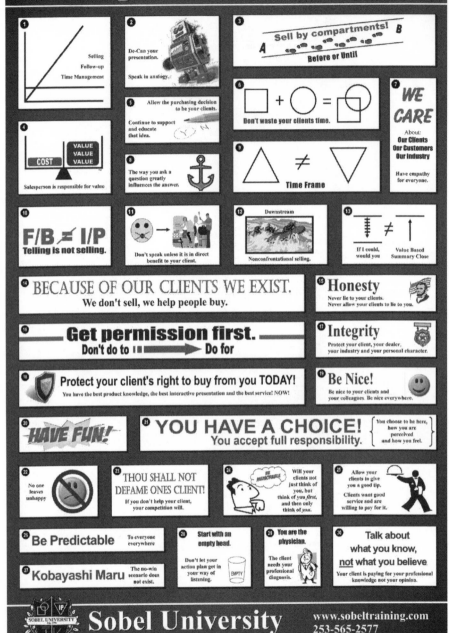

BECAUSE OF OUR CLIENTS WE EXIST.
We don't sell, we help people buy.

Honesty
Never lie to your clients.
Never allow your clients to lie to you.

Get permission first.
Don't do to ▪▪▪ ➡ Do for

Integrity
Protect your client, your dealer,
your industry and your personal character.

Protect your client's right to buy from you TODAY!
You have the best product knowledge, the best interactive presentation and the best service! NOW!

Be Nice!
Be nice to your clients and
your colleagues. Be nice everywhere.

HAVE FUN!

YOU HAVE A CHOICE!
You accept full responsibility.
You choose to be here,
how you are
perceived
and how you feel.

TO ORDER PRINCIPLE CENTERED SELLING POSTERS
FOR YOUR WORKPLACE AND INCREASE RETENTION
OF THE PRINCIPLES CALL 253-565-2577

Principle Centered Selling

Sobel University
www.sobeltraining.com
253-565-2577

READY TO LEARN MORE?
ATTEND ANY 3 OR 5 DAY
COMPREHENSIVE
SALES COURSE
AND RECEIVE 50% OFF THE
NON-CONTRACT RATE.

CALL 253-565-2577 FOR
DATES AND REGISTRATION

Made in the USA
Monee, IL
24 January 2020